TRANSFORMING
A PEOPLE
OF GOD

TRANSFORMING A PEOPLE OF GOD

Denham Grierson

The Joint Board of Christian Education
Melbourne

TRANSFORMING A PEOPLE OF GOD

Published by the Joint Board of Christian Education
Second Floor, 10 Queen Street, Melbourne 3000, Australia

ISBN 0 85819 464 3

First published 1984
Reprinted 1988, 1992

Design: Ron Chandler
Cover: Max Grierson
Typeset by: Davey Graphics
Printed by: The Book Printer
JB92/3266

To the memory of my mother
a bearer of the gift of community
and to the students
of the United Faculty of Theology
and the Evangelical Theological Association
Melbourne
who are the co-authors of this book.

'Now we are of the kind to reach the world of intelligence through the world of sense, since all our knowledge takes its rise from sensation.'
Thomas Aquinas, *Summa Theologiae*, Vol. 1.

'. . . he would do good to others must do it in Minute Particulars; General Good is the place of the Hypocrite and Scoundrel . . .'
William Blake, *Prophetic Books*

'Whatever else modern anthropology asserts . . . it is firm in the conviction that persons unmodified by the customs of particular places do not in fact exist, have never existed, and more important, could not in the very nature of the case exist.'
Clifford Geertz, *The Interpretation of Cultures*

Contents

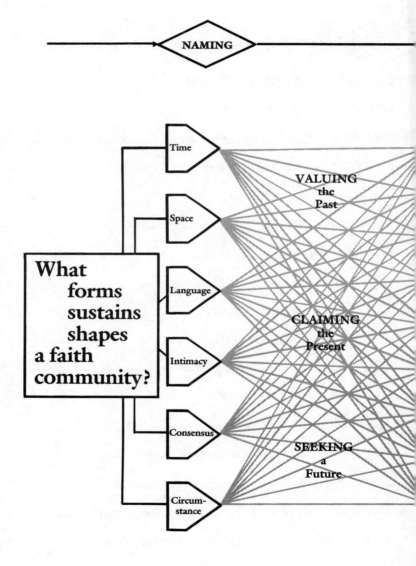

NAMING

Time

Space

Language

Intimacy

Consensus

Circum-
stance

What
forms
sustains
shapes
a faith
community?

VALUING
the
Past

CLAIMING
the
Present

SEEKING
a
Future

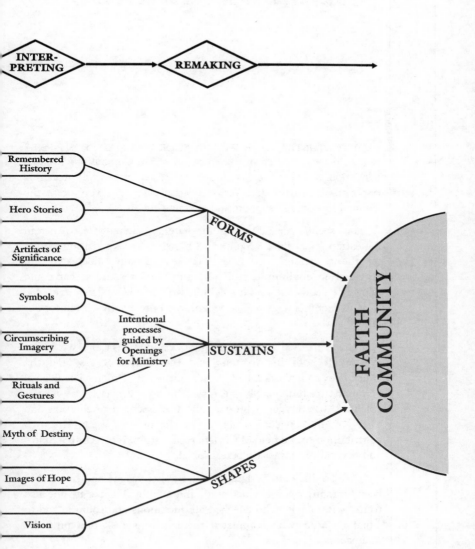

INTER-PRETING → REMAKING →

Remembered History
Hero Stories
Artifacts of Significance

FORMS

Symbols
Circumscribing Imagery
Rituals and Gestures

Intentional processes guided by Openings for Ministry

SUSTAINS

Myth of Destiny
Images of Hope
Vision

SHAPES

FAITH COMMUNITY

7

Acknowledgments

*T*HE OPPORTUNITY TO WRITE THIS BOOK WAS MADE POSSIBLE BY two agencies. The first of these, the Victorian Council of Christian Education, Melbourne, Australia, released me from teaching responsibilities to undertake a sabbatical year. At every point the Council has offered support and encouragement.

The second agency, the Presbyterian School of Christian Education, Richmond, Virginia, U.S.A., where I was a visiting scholar for the academic year 1981-1982, was equally supportive and provided an environment of hospitality and resources that could scarcely be equalled. Faculty, Administration and students made the time in Richmond a singular delight, not only for myself but for our family also.

I have benefited greatly from prolonged conversations with John Westerhoff both in Australia and the United States, and the assistance and wisdom of Sarah Little of Union Theological Seminary, Richmond. My greatest debt, however, is to my former teacher, Ross Snyder, who gave me the essential orientation and many of the concepts which shape the present work. His own contribution to the field of Christian education in the United States and beyond cannot easily be reckoned.

In Australia, Cliff Wright, a long-time colleague and friend, has been for many years a valued guide and mentor. Thanks are due also to my wife Mavis, who checked all quotations and sources, and to Coral Delarue, who completed the laborious task of typing the manuscript.

No acknowledgment would be complete without reference to my own local community of faith, St. Stephen's, or to the rich and varied contribution of the theological communities in Melbourne. Without the students who undertook the task of testing out the ideas here recorded this book could not have been written. It is, as the text reveals clearly enough, not the work of one author but of many. The others, however, bear no blame for the design. If the key does not turn the locks it was designed to open, the fault lies with the locksmith, not the users of the key.

Melbourne, 1983

Preface

THIS BOOK AIMS AT PROVIDING A WAY OF ANSWERING ONE central question. What forms, shapes, sustains a faith community? The term 'faith community' as used refers always to a particular local congregation. The question is in essence a theological question but the perspective taken, while not unmindful of the theological issues, is that of education.

The focus is on providing help to clergy and others, such as teaching elders, who are struggling with the task of educating a particular people of God. It is also concerned with helping theological students as they move from seminary to their first parish, and for those more seasoned pastors who are facing a shift from their present parish to a new one. Those who work in team ministries will find the suggestions offered here of use in seeking a consensual view on the life of their congregations, and in their attempt to discern openings for ministry.

The major assumption about educating a people of God is that it is the culture of the people as a faith community that must be transformed. In order for that to occur, attention must be paid not just to what is apparent and observable but to that which is not evident or visible.

What is recorded here has been tested out over a period of five years by successive students of the United Faculty of Theology and the Evangelical Theological Association in Melbourne, Australia. That includes those from the tradition of Catholic, Anglican, Uniting Church, Baptist, Churches of Christ and Salvation Army churches. The enterprise described has been an ecumenical venture.

Many of the illustrations and stories have come from the attempts of students to use the interpretative framework in field-based activity. The somewhat heroic attempt to forge a master key to the local congregation has been strengthened and refined as more data and experience has been gathered. There is still much refining to do, and in a necessary sense there always will be. The test is whether this particular key can open the doors which lead into the hidden life of a people of God. Such entering-in leads to the possibility of transformation whereby we may escape, through committed involvement, from the dogmatism that teaches us nothing and the scepticism that does not promise anything.

Although what is advanced here does not argue a central thesis of what it means to educate a people of God so much as provide ways of exploring congregational reconstruction and renewal, it suggests a possible statement that can be identified in the following terms: 'To educate a people of God is to call forth a community which by faith seeks to conform its life to the pattern of Christ, and to embody in the style of that life a distinctively Christian confession about human existence'. It is toward such a statement that the project here described seeks to move.

HOW TO READ THIS BOOK

The major focus of this book is the question about the nature of a Christian community and what shapes and sustains it. In seeking an answer to that question six dimensions of analysis are used. These are time: the way a time-sense infuses the life of a congregation; space: the way the people indwell their environment; language: its function in circumscribing the people's reality; intimacy: the forms of its expression among the people; consensus: what is commonly affirmed; and circumstance: the situation in which a congregation struggles to know itself.

Chapter 4 begins the examinaton of the six categories – time, space, language, intimacy, consensus, circumstance – which are foundational for any community. This discussion continues in Chapters 5 and 6.

Chapters 7, 8 and 9 outline interpretative tools and their use, while Chapter 10 identifies the tasks of reconstructing congregational experience with reference to the concerns of liturgy, education, mission and authority. The chart provided diagrams the overall constructs and design of the total schema. The Appendixes are work sheets that can act as a guide for personal action-reflection steps, and group discussion.

The design of the book assumes that the reader is a newcomer to a congregation. For this reason the six identifying categories are placed first to allow time for some familiarity with the environment of the congregation before employing the interpretative suggestions referred to in the text as 'focusing concepts'. Those who have been within a congregation for some time, however, may choose to work with the interpretative tools (Chapters 7, 8 and 9) and then test what is uncovered against the analysis provided by the six categories of analysis.

Although the text suggests a movement from *naming* through *interpretation* to *remaking*, a process of reshaping is implicit in all phases of development. For example, the naming phase is not strictly, or only, a phase of analysis, for the identifying categories shape the perception of the newcomer thus making the interpretation phase possible. Again the first two phases are active in the third phase, remaking, as a substantive element in that process. It is important therefore to perceive that hints for remaking occur all the way through the process and that the total configuration constantly moves forward with all elements in living contact with all other elements.

This story is told with the hope that it may be of help in educating and ministering to a local congregation. It is offered as a guide to those who struggle with the question of how to undertake their ministry. It may also, in a time of disenchantment, help recover a genuine excitement for the service of ministry in a parish setting. The test comes when what is offered here is put to use. Without that action the viability of the suggestions cannot be judged adequately. A key, after all, is for opening doors, not for keeping in one's pocket.

PART ONE
SETTING THE TASK

CHAPTER ONE

The Transitional Crisis

*T*HE QUESTION THAT THIS BOOK ADDRESSES: *WHAT FORMS, shapes, sustains a community of faith?* and the problems it seeks to overcome arose in my early experience of parish life. My first parish was a hydro-electric construction village on the island of Tasmania, a manufactured community of about three thousand people. The town rested on a rocky outcrop five hundred feet above the surrounding pasture lands where cattle and sheep grazed. It lived out its life under the shadow of a vast mountain range through which a mile-long tunnel was being bored to the Great Lake, the source of the water to generate electricity for the future needs of Tasmania.

It was a company town, dominated by its allegiance to one employer, and submissive to its will. The Hydro-Electric Commission of Tasmania owned the land, provided the housing and the jobs, and controlled the lives of the people by its rules and regulations.

The congregation in this small parish was an ecumenical one. The minister or priest served the town on behalf of all church denominations, except Catholic, under the direction of the Tasmanian Council of Churches. Because such towns are thrown up around particular construction projects they last at their peak for only a few years. When the job is done the bulk of the town, including the pre-fabricated housing units, moves on, leaving a small remnant behind to service the power station.

As a consequence there was no secure history of church existence in the parish, no established pattern of worship with one tradition observed above others, no secure guidelines for parish life and structure. A sense of impermanence permeated community life. They were a travelling people.

In such a situation it did not take me long to realise that whatever theological education may have provided by way of preparation for ministry, it had not given me any clear idea of what formed, shaped or sustained a faith community. Perhaps the weight of this discovery would have been less in a more formalised situation where tradition etched out the roles and responsibilities of minister and people. An organised pattern of church life may have obscured the sharpness of the issue.

But in this first exposure to parish life in which there was nothing fixed or final about the life of the people, not even to a secure agreement about the celebration of faith in word and sacrament, this lack in my theological education became starkly apparent. I simply did not know what to do to call this particular community of faith into an understanding of what it was, and yet could be, before God. It was a painful and humiliating discovery. Surely after six years in study and preparation, I told myself, I was equipped to be a minister to this people! The answer to that question was inescapably no!

This lack of an understanding about the sources of Christian community was compounded by another absence in my preparation for the task I had taken up. I had been given no tools of analysis, no guide on how to read the folk culture of those into whose midst I had been placed.

If my first parish was unique in those circumstances which shaped its life, my second parish contributed another variation of the same kind of pattern. Situated on the northern side of the city of Melbourne, the parish comprised two congregations. One of these was a small working class congregation that, at that stage of its life, did not have a professional person in its company. Only seven years old, it was struggling into an identity with a huge debt on its large community hall, and a Sunday school of three hundred children. The congregation that gathered for worship in the small side chapel seldom numbered more than twenty people. The organist travelled from another part of the city so that we might have music at worship.

The people struggled to meet payments on their newly acquired homes. In many cases both parents were engaged in paid employment and had to wrestle with the exhausting problem of raising small children. Unemployment was an ever-present threat. The area had unmade roads, a woefully inadequate public transport system, few community centres or resident doctors.

The second congregation, by contrast, was located in a settled area, boasted a solid brick church building, with flourishing sporting clubs, ladies' guilds, a choir, resident organists and firmly established patterns of church life. The average age of this second congregation was considerably older than that of their sister congregation, and the people seldom crossed over into the new housing area. What succeeded in one place failed miserably in the other. The sources of these different styles of being remained to my untutored gaze eternally elusive.

The parish in which I am presently an associate minister is again quite different. Established and on the south side of Melbourne, the one congregation which comprises the parish has in the recent past called to its pulpit such preachers as would become Moderators of the Presbyterian Assembly or Presidents of the Methodist Conference. Its stately red-brick church is a classified building with the National Trust. A tram runs past the church door, stopping there. No great distance away is one of the most beautiful suburban parks of Melbourne. Sixty-eight percent of the congregation is over the age of sixty-five.

When real estate lists are published the suburb is regularly listed in the top ten for rising property values. Major hospitals, community centres and playing fields dot the municipality. Worship is conducted to the sounds of a magnificent organ and a devoted and well schooled choir.

Sometimes as we break bread and drink wine together, standing at the Lord's table, my mind goes back to the small pre-fabricated church in Tasmania where we had a hand-me-down pedal organ and almost no room for a choir. As colours from the stained glass windows dapple the bread and blur on the silver sheen of the chalice, I remember those churches on the north side of the city where there is no stained glass and the people gather to pray in what is a utility hall.

It is one church, one faith, one family of God as the bread and wine testifies, but painful experience has taught me that the congregations are not the same. In a variety of ways they never will be. At other times and other places the same message has been communicated. A rural parish comes to mind where a goat regularly wandered into the service. Paint, nails and tools were stored in the pulpit. Worship had to stop when the rain on the tin roof made it impossible for the preacher to be heard. Small knots of faithful people in this one geographical area gathered in their church, only five miles from their friends and neighbours gathered in theirs. Try to get them together as one body at your peril!

THE CASE FOR PARTICULARITY

It has been said that three propositions about community are true.

Each community is like every other community.

Some communities are like some other communities.

No community is like any other community.

These propositions about community can be related to the church. All of them have a measure of truth. It is true that wherever a Christian congregation gathers, in whatever form or confessional tradition, it shares central characteristics with every other Christian community: a confession concerning Christ, an acceptance of the normative status of the Scriptures, the practice of prayer, to suggest some.

It is equally the case that some churches, say Anglican, are like other Anglican congregations in significant respects, and different from Salvation Army or Baptist churches in significant respects. Confessional traditions, liturgical style, sacramental practice are different across many Christian denominations. That some congregations are like other congregations remains accurate as a description, just as the negative (and unlike other congregations) is also true.

But what has not been acknowledged strongly enough is the third proposition, the notion that no particular community is like any other. Each community is unique and particular to itself. One cannot be treated the same as another. So many variables exist. Circumstance, quality of leadership, local traditions, style of life, expectations, personal indentity – the list is endless. Each congregation is individual, distinct, unique. It is this proposition that is foundational for what is offered in this book. It is a proposition that generally finds no room in the inns of theological education.

It is axiomatic in seminary that there is one gospel to be preached, one faith to be confessed. An additional unspoken assumption which accompanies this affirmation is that all congregations, insofar as they celebrate the Christian confession, are the same. What is taught therefore in theological centres is assumed to be applicable and transferable without loss or diminution to any local scene. The movement from the culture of theological college or seminary to the culture of a congregation is assumed to be automatic and painless.[1] What one preaches in the college chapel can, with minor adjustment, and the addition of relevant local illustrations, be preached in any local setting.

This assumption is defective at a number of points. It pays no attention to the particularity of culture, and the problem of transferring evident truths from one culture to another where such truths are not evident. As one student wrote with a great deal of passion after a year's exposure to the life of a congregation:

'The seminary gives you an ideal picture of the church – it is difficult in the light of all that we are told about the church to accept what the local congregation is.'

The 'church' so talked about in seminary is neat, tidy, and generally civilised. A particular congregation is never neat, sometimes barely Christian and only rarely civilised. Part of the 'culture shock' is due to the changed status of the student. There is a world of difference between being a member of a congregation, and carrying the weight of its symbolic meaning in the institutionalised role of 'priest', whether that word is understood in a high or low sense. In addition, the student emerging from theological college is a different person from the one who entered. The student who comes to be educated speaking the language and bearing the expectations and world-view of his or her local congregation, is soon stripped of all confidence in their efficacy. This comes through contact with and exposure to a different way of viewing oneself, the 'church' and the 'world'.[2] Much of this is inevitable, even necessary and desirable.

The view of 'the church' which seminary offers is normative, abstract, disembodied. The universal and the particular relate in a most tenuous fashion. Thus the movement from the culture of theological college to the parish is likely to be no less traumatic than the initial movement from the parish into seminary.

It is to this transitional crisis that we now turn in an endeavour to understand it more completely. Four characteristics of that crisis are discussed under the headings of de-tribalisation, transfer, the status of welcomed stranger and reading the culture.

THE TRANSITIONAL CRISIS

1. *De-tribalisation*

As a general rule, candidates for ordination usually come from a deep involvement in a particular parish experience in which they have a clear concept of what it means to be a minister, pastor or priest. They belong with the people, have a secure sense of identity about themselves in that local culture, and because of their participation as indwellers they 'read' the culture through the pores of their skin. It is part of them and they of it, even if they may not be able to say what belonging means with any clarity or coherence. What they know, they know. In a phrase of Michael Polanyi, they know more than they can tell. How they know it is obscure.

When they enter theological college or seminary it is as if the old has passed away. In any case it matters little. The strange new world of theological education will assault all of those centres of worth and significance they bring with them: their sense of identity, their understanding of the ministerial role, their perception and value of the local parish and what is done there. This assault is both direct and indirect, a complex of intentional and accidental factors.

What takes place is a de-tribalisation process that is alarming to some, threatening to most, and determinative for all. An analogy might help to underscore this transformation. When a recruit joins the army, he is stripped of civilian identification and given a uniform, subjected to a battery of tests of a most impersonal kind, has his hair cut to a required length and is re-educated in his understanding of authority, discipline and personal responsibility. He becomes different. In a less dramatic way, although nonetheless discernible to the practised eye, the candidate for ordination is remade in the process of being theologically educated whether he or she understands it or not. What is often lost in that remaking is a sense of where they have come from, and what it means to be 'of the people'. Much of this change is inevitable. It can be almost fatal for the exercise of ministry, as John M'biti records.

'He learned German, Greek, French, Latin, Hebrew, in addition to English, church history, systematics, homiletics, exegesis, and pastoralia, as one part of the requirements for his degree. The other part, the dissertation, he wrote on some obscure theologian of the Middle Ages. Finally, he got what he wanted: a Doctorate in Theology. It took him nine and a half years altogether, from the time he left his home until he passed his orals and set off to return. He was anxious to reach home as soon as possible, so he flew, and he was glad to pay for his excess baggage which, after all, consisted only of the Bible in the various languages he had learned, plus Bultmann, Barth, Bonhoeffer, Brunner, Buber, Cone, Kung, Moltmann, Niebuhr, Tillich, *Christianity Today, Time Magazine* . . .

'At home, relatives, neighbours, old friends, dancers, musicians, drums, dogs, cats, all gather to welcome him back. The fatted calves are killed; meat is roasted; girls giggle as they survey him surrounded by his excess baggage; young children have their imaginations rewarded – they had only heard about him but now they see him; he, of course, does not know them by name. He must tell about his experiences overseas, for everyone has come to eat, to rejoice, to listen, to their hero who has studied so many northern languages, who has read so many theological books, who is the hope of their small but fast-growing church, the very incarnation of theological learning. People bear with him patiently as he struggles to speak his own language, as occasionally he seeks the help of an interpreter from English. They are used to sitting down and making time; nobody is in a hurry; speech is not a matter of life or death. Dancing, jubilation, eating, feasting – all these go on as if there is nothing else to do, because the man for whom everyone had waited has finally returned.

'Suddenly there is a shriek. Someone has fallen to the ground. It is his older sister, now a married woman with six children and still going strong. He rushes to her. People make room for him, and watch him. "Let's take her to the hospital," he calls urgently. They are stunned. He becomes quiet. They all look at him bending over her. Why doesn't someone respond to his advice? Finally a schoolboy says, "Sir, the nearest hospital is 50 miles away, and there are few buses that go there." Someone else says, "She is possessed. Hospitals will not cure her!" The chief says to him. "You have been studying theology overseas for 10 years. Now help your sister. She is troubled by the spirit of her great aunt." He looks around. Slowly he goes to get Bultmann, looks at the index, finds what he wants, reads again about spirit possession in the New Testament. Of course he gets the answer: Bultmann has demythologized it. He insists that his sister is not possessed. The people shout, "Help your sister; she is possessed!" He shouts back, "But Bultmann has demythologized demon possession." (This story is entirely fictional and is not based on the experience of a real person.)'[3]

If John M'biti's story seems exaggerated it is only because the home setting in Africa and the centres of theological education in Europe are so culturally and geographically distinct. Yet within the same society the movement from one sub-culture to another is just as distinct. You need travel no further than around the block in some cities to enter a different world, where to belong requires a radical relearning. It involves the acquisiton of a different language, determining symbols, folk truths, unifying myths; in short a redefinition of the taken-for-granted realities of the world.[4]

M'biti is clear that the church is both kerygmatically universal and theologically provincial. The next phase of the transition crisis supports that proposition. It is the dynamic associated with transferring from one cultural ethos to another that defines the next step.

2. *Transfer*

The issue of transfer is not new.[5] Theological education in the 1960-70s sought to deal with the problem of transfer from school to parish in two ways. The first was the burgeoning of doctoral programs which were directed to the professional practice of ministry. The second was to supplement theory courses in traditional curricula with a variety of practical courses which were intended to create a bridge between academia and the parish. The theoria-praxis debate continues undiminished into the 1980s.[6] But the increasing doubts about the effectiveness of the attempts made to bring seminary and parish into conversation with each other often fail to recognise that the problem of transfer of learning is related not only to the foreground questions of what is theory and what is practice but to the background factors of the cultural environment in which learning takes place. As John Dewey argued, the most effective education occurs not directly but indirectly by means of the environment.

The cultural environment is as determinative in the formation of images for ministry as the formal content offered in classes. What is not present is, in a sense, as crucial as what is present. Theological education, as a generalisation, has a proper and determined commitment to library, chapel and lecture room as the foci of educational pursuits. It does not give sufficient attention in the formation of patterns of ministry to what is communicated by the absence of dialogue with lay people in the locale of the parish environment. Who we are and how we come to know ourselves is partly a function of where we are.

The process being described here is not just a critical appropriation of the traditions of a particular theological community. It is the internalisation of images of what it means to be a minister, with its resident assumptions about authority, style, status, and priorities

The assumption, already noted, is that these traditions (most powerful at the tacit level) can be learned in their pure form, abstracted and divorced from their particular expression in a local gathering of people who together struggle to live a life of faith. Yet the understanding of faithful living of a local community is inevitably shaped by the unique and peculiar events of its own life.

What is learned in separation in one cultural setting therefore does not necessarily transfer with meaning to another. It is difficult not to overstate the case, for clearly much that is learned in theological college is essential and can be usefully employed in the practice of ministry. That is not at issue. The claim here is that what is intrinsic to the practice of ministry is embedded in a cultural matrix and decisively shaped by it. That cultural enfolding is crucial in developing and sanctioning patterns for ministry. It is as persuasive as much in the way it teaches as in what is taught.

Much learning theory research has been directed to maximising the chances of what is learned in one environment being transferred positively to another. The results generally sustain what experience teaches; that is, that the greater the similarity of the task and environment in which learning takes place to the environment in which the skills will be subsequently employed, the greater the chance of an adequate transfer of learning. It is more than a matter of skill however. It includes the integration of what has been learned so that the parts merge into a balanced whole.

To illustrate this latter point of integration of learning, or more particularly, a failure of integration of learning, a group of students was given the passage in the New Testament of the encounter between Zacchaeus and Jesus with the task of communicating its essential message to a group of five-year-olds. They concluded that what they would share with the children was that Zacchaeus was a lonely person and Jesus cares for us when we are lonely. Afterwards when they were questioned it was revealed that they had not asked of the text any of those questions which they had been taught in New Testament exegesis (such questions as: what was the purpose of the writer in recording this passage?, what of its setting?, its theological significance?). They had completed the task without reference to those tools taught in another stream of their educational experience. This illustration is characteristic of learning systems where little or no attention is paid to the integration of learning, or the transfer of what is learned into different environments.

These elements, the expectations that interpenetrate the learning environment, the learning of an orientation to ministry in separation from the environment in which ministry will occur, and the failure to achieve a comprehensive integration of what is learned, are all part of the problem of transfer. It is not unknown for some students to heave a sigh of relief upon leaving seminary for they have only been able to survive by remaining strangers within its walls. What guides their practice of ministry subsequently has its roots in what they believed before they entered theological education. The movement into the heavily rational environment of theological college is, for them, a most painful experience. The movement out of seminary is one of relief. Most however, if they indwell the ethos of a theological college to a significant degree, confront the problem of transfer most directly upon leaving the seminary.

What occurs when no attention is paid to this issue of transfer is what occurred in my own case. This was an uncritical movement of the truths acquired in a distinct but separate cultural setting into another distinct cultural setting which did not share the same orientation, values or consensus about authority or church life. There are few theological centres unaware of this problem. It can fairly be said that only a small number of such centres have developed creative solutions to bridge the gap between school and parish. The problem of transfer remains largely unresolved.

3. *Welcomed stranger*

The status of the ordained person within a congregation is taken for granted in most situations. Whether perceived in terms of role performance or that of symbol bearer of the life of the congregation, the newly arrived ordained person is welcomed in terms of place and status into the centre of the worshipping community. That centrality is one of functional and liturgical necessity. The person so welcomed is nonetheless a stranger to that deep sensibility by which a particular congregation understands and identifies itself.[7]

Any stranger who approaches a new culture does so in an ambivalent fashion. From the side of the congregation he or she is both a bearer of gifts and an unknown threat to their accustomed patterns of behaviour. The stranger, for his or her part, is also uncertain about what will be tolerated and what will not.

This marginal position enables the stranger to see what those living within the taken-for-granted life of the parish cannot see. It is a salutary lesson to learn that the taken-for-granted reality of the parish is complex, ambiguous, often self-contradictory and far from coherent. What appears on the surface as random does have point and meaning from the perspective of those who belong in the deep structure of the congregation's life.

Again what appears to be the case upon the surface is not necessarily the case. In one parish a prolonged conflict occurred over the practice of the ladies' guild of placing a vase of flowers on the communion table. The new minister, on the basis of sound theological principles and an impeccable liturgical viewpoint well supported in theological college, made strenuous efforts to remove them.

The conflict proved to be an illustration of two world views passing each other. The practice had arisen in the particular congregation positively as a confession of God's grace in renewing the world daily, and negatively because of the attempt of a former minister to close the women's group down. A vase of flowers was, to the women's group, a symbol both of their identity as a group and a confession of their faith as Christians.

The new minister saw only a custom he could not affirm with integrity. That was all he saw, and before his outlook had become informed much damage had been done to the life of the parish. Similar stories can be told about attempts to remove national flags from churches, or to change the arrangement of church furniture bearing brass plates in honour of deceased parents and grandparents.

Some conflict is inevitable. The 'gods of the tribe' are not necessarily the gods of the newcomer. Much that is held as holy may well be spurned and violated unwittingly. To learn involves a new belonging. The delicate balance between acting as the public agent of the culture, with appropriate sensitivity to local custom, and being a person with one's own taken-for-granted view of reality, fashioned by participation in and loyalty to another community, is seldom maintained consistently and without compromise. At its worst the interaction can result in estrangement. At best a creative interchange occurs, in which both parties reach a comfortable agreement and seek new possibilities together.

Success in one congregation does not ensure success in the next. I remember vividly the anguish and bewilderment of a gifted minister who, after years of deeply satisfying service to one people, found that in his new congregation little that he offered was accepted, although it had brought his previous parish alive. He felt he was the same person with the same skills. So he was. But he transgressed deeply held norms in his new congregation without knowing it. When he found out, the situation was beyond recovery. He moved on, disillusioned with the parish and doubting himself.

The marginal nature of the newcomer inevitably involves a conflict of loyalty which often centres on the gap between that image of the church held 'in absoluta' and what the local congregation actually is. Is one's primary loyalty to a vision of the church as biblically derived and theologically normative? Or is it to serving a particular people, which means sitting lightly to many substantive theological issues that arise daily around such issues as baptism, abortion, mothers' day services, use of the church buildings by the 'eastern meditation and karate group' and the practice of Christian burial in the secular environment of the undertaker's parlour? These options are in constant tension and may appear mutually exclusive in their daily appearance.

Few of these issues are resolved absolutely. They take on a particular form in a concrete local setting. And to begin with (if not longer than that) the particular cultural shape of a local congregation is as opaque as travelled ice on the surface of a pond. How to see into the depths? How to read the culture accurately? These are questions every newcomer confronts in the phase of transition.

4. *Reading the culture*

If we plan to travel into unknown territory it is usual to seek a map that gives us some idea of what we are likely to encounter on the journey ahead. Information on climate can be obtained. Reports are available that describe the state of the roads. Thus equipped, it is possible to proceed with a measure of confidence that when certain features of the unknown countryside are encountered they will have a measure of familiarity about them. In addition, resources can be identified that will serve in an emergency and preparation made to carry those necessary items which will come into their own as the need arises.

The analogy of the journey helps to illustrate what much of theological education attempts to do. As far as possible, advice and guidance are offered that will bring the movement from seminary to parish existence to a creative resolution. Where such efforts are conscientiously observed much that is valuable is gained.

But much that is essential is not available through the most careful of briefing, preparation or wise counsel. To return to the map illustration, no map can possibly help with those encounters with people and events which make any journey significant. A knowledge of the physical characteristics of the new land to be visited is of limited value. What is critical, an existential knowledge of events and circumstances, is only available in direct contact with the people. Such encounters imply risk and uncertainty. To understand it is necessary to ask for guidance and be instructed by the people themselves. Arguing from a guide-book about what the situation should be is less than helpful.

When one enters the culture of a congregation the requirements of naming, understanding and interpreting what is there cannot be fulfilled by reference to the generalised wisdom that can be gathered before one enters the life world of the parish. The networks of communication, the formative events, the deeply held sentiments that shape the consciousness and identity of the people are not available to the onlooker or observer. It is also true that the deep structure of meaning that sustains the life of the people is beyond the people's capacity to articulate clearly. The webs of significance are as invisible as the air we breathe and as fragile as childhood memories of lost parents.

How is the newcomer to read the signs of the hidden sources of meaning and significance which constitute the people as a community of faith? The reading of that culture includes appreciation of the rhythm of shared life, the codes of conduct which set limits to what is acceptable, and the ritual gestures which reveal where the hidden treasure of collective existence is stored. The tools offered by sociology and anthropology are useful, but limited. For the inner life of a Christian community is circumscribed by faith and guided by its expression. To understand a Christian community one has to share the faith it confesses, for faith itself is a way of knowing. To minister to a faith community one needs to be able to say clearly what is received confusedly from the people.[8] For in the retelling of the story they know, and the journey they live, the people are renewed again. They hear the story as if for the first time, and claim its promise and responsibility afresh.

In summary therefore, what has been described is the need for ways of understanding a culture that facilitates a ready appreciation of the customs and traditions of a particular parish. The transition from theological school to a parish brings its own crisis. The newly appointed minister has internalised expectations and images of himself or herself in roles that are not shared by the people to be served.

The complex processes of de-tribalisation, the difficulties of transferring to a new environment, and the ambiguities associated with the status of welcomed stranger, call for ways of helping people understand what is happening to them. To do this they must have resources to read the new situation into which they move.

What is true in the movement from seminary to parish is true for the movement from parish to parish. The status of the stranger to an unknown culture is always one of both threat and promise. In describing the difficulty of transition there is an assumption that, to overcome it creatively, the total configuration of the parish must be addressed as an organic whole. The reasons for that judgment are now to be explored.

NOTES TO CHAPTER 1

1. The word 'culture' is capable of infinite definition it seems. It is used here in a restricted sense to apply to the life of a particular congregation, and the particular patterns of identity and purpose that emerge from the complex of relationships which constitute the congregation as an organic whole. The congregation is interpenetrated by the influences, values and expectations of other cultural forces than its own, whether local, regional, state or national characteristics. These levels of cultural reality are not denied in the way the word culture is used, only given a diminished focus in order that the life of the congregation can be taken as the starting point for ethnographic reflection.

2. What is being described is a process associated generally with the move into higher education. For example, and by way of contrast, the comment of Gwen Neville on the training of ethnographers:

'Part of the training of the ethnographer-ethnologist is the subjection of the person during graduate study to a rigorous reprogramming through which the customs, habits, beliefs, etc., of the scholarly and scientific community are substituted for those of an individual's own cultural community of orientation.'

From *Learning Through Liturgy*, by Gwen Kennedy Neville and John H. Westerhoff III. Copyright© 1978 by The Seabury Press, Inc. Used with permission.

3. M'biti, John S. 'Theological Importance and the Universality of the Church', pp 6-8, *Mission Trends No. 3*, edited by Gerald H. Anderson and Thomas F. Stransky G.S.P., Paulist Press, N.Y., Ramsey, Toronto, and Wm. B. Eerdmans Publishing Co., Grand Rapids, 1976. Used by permission.

4. Chaim Potok's novel *The Chosen* illustrates how an ancient yet living tradition can exist as a separate religious sub-culture within a large, secular modern city. The tension of inter and cross-cultural living are graphically present in all his novels and sharpen the concept of what is here referred to as 'de-tribalisation'.

5. A research study called *Crossing the Boundary* undertaken by the Alban Institute in consultation with parish clergy documents the problems of transfer in considerable detail. Their comprehensive suggestions on how to deal with the problems identified offer an alternative and complementary viewpoint to that taken in this book. The issue of the 'culture' of the congregation is not addressed in the recommendations in *Crossing the Boundary*. See *Crossing the Boundary* Between Seminary and Parish, Roy M. Oswald, The Alban Institute Inc. Mount St. Alban, Washington D.C. 20016, 1980.

6. For an extended discussion of the history of developments in theological education over this period see *Theological Education*, Spring 1981, Vol. XVII, No. 2.

7. An illuminating discussion of this phenomenon is contained in an essay by Alfred Schulz, 'The Stranger: an essay in Social Psychology', *Studies in Social Theory*, ed. A. Brodersen, The Hague, Martinus Nijhoff, 1964. It is not always the case that a new minister is welcomed. Grief at the loss of the former minister needs to be successfully negotiated. If it is not, it can take the form of hostility to the newcomer, at least initially.

8. This concept of the task of leadership was held by Chairman Mao. '. . . we must teach the masses clearly what we have received from them confusedly', Mao Tse Tung, quoted in *Pedagogy of the Oppressed*, by Paolo Freire, New York, Herder and Herder, 1970, footnote 7, p.82.

CHAPTER TWO

Philosophical Orientation

*H*UMAN BEINGS ARE CAPTIVES OF THEIR CULTURE, BECAUSE IT IS
the dimension of culture that shapes and fashions our humanness.
According to William Hall from 'birth we learn the silent language
of our own culture, what to notice, how to use time and space, how
to use our voice and our body, even how close to stand and how to
breathe'.[1] The life of the church is not free from the currents of social
creation. Such an admission should not be regarded with dismay.

In *Treasure in Earthen Vessels* James Gustafson argues that the
historical and social relativity of the church is part of its essential
character. 'The church can be defined as a human community with
an historical continuity identifiable by certain beliefs, ways of work,
rites, loyalties, outlooks, and feelings.'[2] The local congregation is a
curious mixture of the universal and the particular. On the one hand
there is the celebration of worship and the eucharist that have their
appearance in every place Christians gather. On the other there are
the quirks and idiosyncrasies that give a special character to each
local and particular community. People live into, cherish and protect
the signs of their identity and their history. As Richard Niebuhr
writes, '. . . every community is a particular thing, the product of its
own past and the possessor of a limited culture'.[3] All of this is to
describe a human process that becomes personal and binding in the
inner life of a community. The life of a community by its very nature
teaches many things.

This is essentially the case with a faith community that clusters
around its generative symbolic centres as a beehive swarms around
its queen bee. The intense organic system of relatedness that results
has unique originative depth for each congregation: unique in its
differences, originative through the participative engagement of the

people in shared activities. The enterprises they undertake make sense to them because they are expressive of who they are and what they profess.

The problem we have identified is: How does the stranger who comes to serve as minister or priest enter into the rich symbolic life of the congregation? How does he or she link up with the creative energies, as invisible as radio waves, that connect the life force of the community in its self-awareness? How does the stranger at the gate enter in and find a home? And what guides them in their attempt to answer the question: 'What forms, shapes, sustains a community of faith?'

DEFINING THE STARTING POINT

The preference for an empirical starting point is implicit in what has been said about culture. Such a starting point is necessary if the discipline of education with its inherent demands is to guide any answer which is proffered for consideration. Such an orientation can claim as a warrant for its arguments the work of cultural anthropologists, philosophers in the tradition of Husserl and the phenomenologists, and sociologists committed to the sociology of knowledge. Support also comes from educators such as John Dewey who sought a philosophy of education based on a philosophy of experience, psychologists such as Jung, Freud, Rank and Adler, geneticists concerned with the basic stuff of life, D.N.A. and the mysteries of the human brain, as well as theologians ancient and modern.[4]

A strong consensus about the influence of culture in the shaping of human consciousness overlaps the boundaries of many fields of inquiry. Certainly within the human sciences it is generally acknowledged that knowledge of the self, and the perspective of the self in relation to its sustaining community, is relative to the particular human environment that nourishes it.

The impact of this understanding has long been felt in the field of religious education, through a group of theorists that includes Horace Bushnell, George Coe, Harrison Elliot in its earliest expression, and particularly Ellis Nelson, John Westerhoff and Bernard Martaler in the contemporary scene. Of the many perspectives possible the socialisation process is regarded as the most critical factor in the nurturing and forming of a faith perspective, and the most satisfying explanation of how faith is birthed and sustained.

Socialisation, that process by which we are nurtured into a particular view of reality by interaction with a particular group of people, is not of itself sufficient explanation for the persisting occurrence of faith. Its supporters argue that it cannot be neglected as a persuasive explanation of how faith is formed and seeks expression in varying cultural settings.

Ellis Nelson, whose book, *Where Faith Begins*, is a classic statement of what is known as the socialisation theory of religious education, argues that within the embrace of a faith community personal identity, world view and value orientation are given shape and direction. 'My thesis is that faith is communicated by a community of believers and that the meaning of faith is developed by its members out of their history, by their interaction with each other, and in relation to the events that take place in their lives.'[5] John Westerhoff who shares much the same perspective affirms that faith can only be nurtured within a self-conscious intentional community of faith.[6] Just as Schleiermacher sought to construct a theology that gave expression to the believing experience of the church, this stream in the religious education movement focuses on the organic relationship between faith development and the Christian community. What is helpful in this orientation is that it links theological reflection, liturgical expression, education and the Christian community together in an indissoluble unity.[7]

HOW DOES A COMMUNITY EDUCATE

In the present body of material on faith as socialisation however there is a significant lack which Thomas Groome identifies with precision.

'But none of them (socialization theorists) has shown how intentional education within the community can be enhanced by socialization but also a corrective to undesirable socializing influences . . .They are perceptive in explaining how the whole Christian community educates but are not nearly as clear on how the community can be educated.'[8]

Groome makes further telling criticisms of the socialisation perspective which generally are recognised and acknowledged by the proponents of this view. The most telling is the inbuilt conservative assumption about uncritically accepting the values of a particular sub-culture. Such value formation can be mis-educative from a Christian perspective, and blind to the sharp prophetic dimension in the biblical tradition. Equally damaging is the passivity engendered in relation to issues of social justice outside the community's life. We will have reason to return to this criticism in chapter 10. For the present it is sufficient to acknowledge the force of Groome's attack on the lack of clarity about how a culture can be educated and to add a further comment to his critical stance.

The life of a local congregation cannot unambiguously be equated with a faith community as defined. There are normative elements in all such definitions which theology affirms as present in but not identified with the gathering of people in any place.

That restraint which theology requires means that general propositions about a faith community or the church are the only statements that can be made. No matter how much we admire the beauty and uniqueness of the individual snow-flake, we are only able to talk with integrity about snow!

Such statements as can be made about the church are prescriptive in nature, not descriptive. This leads to a situation in which a particular local congregation can only be affirmed as a faith community in the most tentative fashion. So scrupulous does this theological imperative become that what is left is some faint hope that the congregation might, in some manner hidden and undefined, represent a people of God, although such a position cannot be maintained with any degree of certainty. The ghost of Docetus continues to haunt the naves and chancels of the land.

Educators in the church cannot afford to be so objective. Nor can parish clergy. Each Sunday a group of people gathers to confess itself as part of the body of Christ, broken and inadequate though it is. This present existential social reality has to be taken with full seriousness, without avoiding in any degree the responsibility it represents. How can this fragile human community grow to be more completely that which it confesses itself to be? What processes are available, which have sound theological credentials as well as educational integrity, to enable a particular congregation become what in Christ it is?

In seeking to answer these questions the general stance outlined above in relation to the decisive influence of the congregation in the formation of faith is judged to be most helpful. It will be necessary subsequently to modify the loyalty given to that particular body of opinion by claiming other guides. But the basic orientation remains persuasive. In a sense the history of religious education this century has made it inevitable. Priority has moved from educating children in faith through the Sunday school, to ministry to youth witnessed by the proliferation of youth departments in major denominations, then to work with adults, and now to inter-generational programming. The focus on such a foreground has long obscured the background significance of the congregation as a total system. It is the whole which gives meaning to the parts, rather than the parts to the whole. Perhaps we now have the security of asking the central question about faith and its formation in a context appropriate to the church's present need.

SOME BASIC ASSUMPTIONS

Several assumptions follow from affirming the perspective referred to as the socialisation stream in the contemporary religious education scene.

1. The local congregation is the primary focus of the educational process.

2. To educate christianly, the culture of the congregation needs to be addressed as a whole (not disparate parts of it).

3. The inner history of the congregation is the key to understanding the outward expression of its life.

The last assumption needs further elaboration in order to appreciate its force.

Each local congregation can be viewed as a complex reality in which the outer and inner dimensions of its life are integrated with each other. The hidden depth of the people's shared life is not necessarily integrated with its outer expression in an immediate or unambiguous way. It follows that, to a newcomer, the nature and meaning of the inner life of the congregation is unveiled by a variety of unexpected means. Much that is encountered is puzzling. Only by participation in the life of the people does the newcomer gain access to the central events and convictions that interpret the data he or she seeks to understand.

OUTER AND INNER DIMENSIONS

The outer reality of the congregation includes what is visibly there. It can have the same outward appearance as other communities that the newcomer knows. The characteristics shared in common with other communities include a group of people gathered together in one place with sufficient agreement among them to invest their corporate acts with a special significance. The common life, expressed in word and act, is directed to the celebration of a relationship with an unseen presence. The people gather regularly with a central recurring pattern of events, varied in detail according to particular need or circumstance, but always anchored by a deeply embedded fidelity to accepted tradition.

The inner reality of the same group of people corresponds to this outer pattern with appropriate correlation between word, event and corporate meaning. The central structure of the shared inner life includes a view of Christ and the confession of him as Lord, the one who reveals the nature and purpose of God for humankind. The regular gatherings remember those who have shared the same faith commitment but are now dead. They are honoured by their devotion to the same vision of God. The language of the people is replete with images of God that come from experience and the central confession that binds them together with past history: God as Father, Mother, King, Shepherd, Saviour, Pioneer, Judge, Deliverer and many others. Each congregation makes selective and judicious use of some out of a vast array of metaphors about the Divine.

The actions of the people usually (but not always in all denominational traditions) includes the breaking of bread and the drinking of wine as well as the baptism of its members. These visible symbols draw on the deep and profound complex of meanings that define their faith, once delivered to the saints and now alive in them. Help is sought in the present to deal with a range of assaults on human life, disease, natural disaster, broken relationships, wars and death, and for strength to remain firm in their commitment until the end of the human journey.

It is this mythic structure that gives a pattern to the culture of the congregation. Each particular culture consists of related elements which are organised into a general configuration by obedience to central determining events and concepts. This patterning provides orientation for those who live within its influence, interpreting for them the meaning of their lives. Participation in such a community means that the indweller is formed by the corporate world view in which shared images and ideas are learned in a complex inter-weaving of relationships and sustained by the repetition of focal words and ritual events within a general framework of meaning.

Social patterns change slowly, and in a small community they are responsive to the inner logic of the common story of the people. Within a congregation there may be variant understandings of what that story is. Equally, the essential dynamic of the story can be lost so that the ritual celebration of that story becomes formal and empty. But where a sense of the people's story lives, it vivifies their life. The dynamic of the story gives vibrancy to the networks of communication that sustain the sense of being one people.

To understand means to enter into the resident belief systems in order to appreciate their power and to know what they mean. Only in that way is an understanding gained of how the inner and outer aspects of the life of the people are fused and interpenetrate each other.[9]

CULTURE

When the word 'culture' is used to refer to a particular people, it is referring to the unique shape, flow and style of a local congregation. It means the patterned way of life produced by a people through which its members are formed and shaped by the manner of their belonging. Belonging gives substance to their personal identity and what they value, to their style of life and what it confesses, and to their ways of acting and what they purpose to accomplish.

FAITH AND CULTURE

The enterprise of understanding the local congregation from within its own self-understanding is one in which the resources of theology and education need to be united. If theology is belief-ful conversation that arises from the corporate experiences of the Christian community, then a proper focus of its concern is the life-matrix of a local congregation struggling to live by faith.

This orientation of theological thinking to the faith community is in agreement with Schleiermacher's claim that theological thinking is reflection upon and clarification of believing experience.[10] It involves disciplined and critical thinking, as well as a unitive style of doing theology which is concerned with its responsibility to guide the common life shared by believers. There are other sources of Christian self-understanding that claim recognition, but what is being explored here is an attempt to undertake theological work from the belief-ful experience of the local congregation, in the first instance. Necessary corrections to what is encountered must be made with appropriate reference to tradition, scripture and dogmatic formulation.

But the initial step is the attempt to struggle with the 'unmediated experience' of a most precise, particular community, and to seek to appreciate the sense in which such a community can claim to be the body of Christ. It is an attempt to identify what is given to, and in, the experience of the people as Gift; and to make it visible, in the most direct way possible, in present historical circumstances. It is a particular form of Niebuhr's assertion: '. . . we can proceed only by stating in simple, confessional form what has happened to us in our community, how we came to believe, how we reason about things and what we see from our point of view.'[11]

The outcome envisaged is a process by which a fuller and richer expression of Christian experience is embodied and made manifest through the culture of a particular congregation, both at the level of conscious awareness and in the style of life the congregation lives.

FAITH

Faith is understood to be that believing commitment to the action of God in Christ which persists in a local congregation and gives it character, direction and possibilities for new futures. Faith has an enduring focus in its christological confession and takes its form in the cultural realities in which it comes to expression. That is, faith is shaped by the particular events of a precise historical period, events which become normative in the life of the people in terms of identity and destiny. Nonetheless faith, despite its outer garments, is never wholly contained nor circumscribed by the moods and fashions of cultural circumstances.

The function of faith within a culture is to give it a depth which rescues the people from superficial interpretations of their Christian journey. Further, faith is the source of a sense of meaning and power that derives from happenings and configurations of events that are deeper than consciousness. Bernard Meland in his book *Faith and Culture* provides an intriguing idea for defining what is intended here when he argues for what he calls 'the structure of experience'.

In a community which can name itself as a community, according to Meland, there is a feeling dimension which forms itself into structural depths. This structural depth in the community gives character to the conscious level of personality and culture, a feeling context he refers to as 'the structure of experience.'

'The structure of experience in any culture is the nurturing context of meanings, feelings, and valuations through which the past is transmitted and emerging events are qualitatively formed. It is, in a general sense, the source of all actualized meaning and value insofar as these are internalized by persons; and it is the carrier of much more that persists as in a social protoplasm – potential, but never actualized in personalized existence.'[12]

If the latent seminal meanings that are contained in the structure of experience are to be appropriated there must be a conscious effort made to give expression to them. The subtle meanings and evaluations of the congregation can only be given full expression when they are owned. Then through engagement and reflection they can be possessed as that generative source which forms and shapes what the congregation is.

The task of education, when addressed to the total expression of the congregation's life, is one of calling forth, even calling out, that which is known in the depth of the people's life. In that way, through shared conversation, the collective wisdom of the community can be affirmed and celebrated.

It has already been acknowledged that the task so described needs to be theologically as well as educationally grounded. Part of the difficulty in forging a joint enterprise between theology and education is that much theological thinking has lifted faith out of the feeling context which the structure of experience represents. Such theology has largely become a history of what theologians have thought. This kind of theological thinking does not, in any significant way, make contact with contemporary experience. If faith is to give birth to deepened awareness and transforming power in the lives of the people it must learn to name itself in its local, particular taken-for-granted reality.[13]

This is to take a position which claims that the presence of Grace is to be detected in ordinary, every-day events. Grace is to be sought and acknowledged in the commonplace happenings of a congregation's life. Transformation can be expected, not in some other realm of experience, but in that moment when the outer expression of the congregation's life melds with its inner determining myth. The separation of daily life and ritual existence is overcome by the recognition of God in the midst.

SUMMARY

The movement to re-creation is not just in an isolated sector of the community but infuses the whole of the community's life. A community of faith is to be understood as an interconnected system in which the parts participate as a growing, living organism. What the congregation intends itself to be as a worshipping, believing, serving community has some chance of coming to incarnational expression when the focus of educating is the collective life of the people, an emerging continuing obedient response to its own inner depths. Christ, as Bonhoeffer claimed, takes form in a band of men and women. If ways of calling a congregation into new life are fed on that vision of Christ-among-us, we are not so easily tempted to ignore the local congregation and to look for signs of the presence and action of God elsewhere. The hope expressed for the congregation's renewal is not one that simply reinforces the old. It is rather believing that in the old lies buried the seed of the new, waiting to burst forth in such strength as to overcome ambiguity and doubt, and proclaim in its very appearing that which it truly is.

Because the congregation's life is always in process, it is not be be expected that any sequence of events will define its life absolutely. There can be no premature closure on the journey. But to travel with hope and a measure of understanding is possible. To feel and touch again the 'well-spring of desire' is to know that through the commonplace the uncommon shines, that paradoxically the very brokenness of our life is the precondition for announcing it restored. The existence the congregation shares gives testimony to its essential nature through the symbols, stories and myths that are offered again and again as the source of faith. Such faith in search of understanding can find itself renewed again by the faithful telling of the story they know to be true yet forget again and again.

NOTES TO CHAPTER 2

1. Hall, William. 'Your Country Matters' in *Psychology Today*, Vol 2 No. 10. Interview with Elizabeth Hall, English edition, p.30.

2. Gustafson, James. *Treasure in Earthen Vessels: the church as a human community*, New York: Harper, 1961, p.3.

Gustafson is affirming what Troeltsch wrote before him. Ernst Troeltsch, *The Social Teaching of the Christian Churches*, Vol. I, II, London: George Allen and Unwin Ltd., New York: The Macmillan Company, 1931, see Vol. 1, p.31.

3. Niebuhr, H. Richard. *The Meaning of Revelation*, p.15. Reprinted with permission of Macmillan Publishing Company from *The Meaning of Revelation* by H. Richard Niebuhr. Copyright 1941 by Macmillan Publishing Company, Inc., renewed 1969 by Florence Niebuhr, Cynthia M. Niebuhr and Richard R. Niebuhr. Note Niebuhr's comment on the sphere where revelation is to be found: 'That sphere is internal history, the story of what happened to us, the living memory of the community.' (p.90) He means here of course more than a local community but a local community is certainly included in the sphere of revelation.

4. It is possible to give an extended list to support this contention. However, in the field of theology the empirical perspective is most represented by the tradition of the Chicago school, the present representatives of which are Langdon Gilkey and David Tracy, both influenced by Paul Tillich. A book such as Harvey Cox's *The Seduction of the Spirit* returns to an appreciation of the small church environment.

For a sociologist's argument for an empirical starting point for theology see Peter Berger, *The Heretical Imperative*, Garden City, New York: Anchor Press, 1979.

5. *Where Faith Begins*, by C. Ellis Nelson, p.10. Copyright M.E. Bretcher 1967. Published by John Knox Press. Used by permission.

6. Westerhoff III, John. *Will Our Children Have Faith?* New York: The Seabury Press, 1976.

7. Many of those who belong to the Catholic and Orthodox traditions have always held that it is the liturgy that teaches. Education in faith therefore is substantially viewed as preparing people for meaningful participation in worship.

8. Groome, Thomas. *Christian Religious Education*, San Francisco: Harper and Row, 1980, p.126. Published in Australia by Dove Communications. Used by permission.

9. If anyone has had the experience of an outer tread of a car tyre becoming separated from its inner base, they will appreciate the impossibility of moving the car forward. Similarly when the rituals and external acts of a congregation become separated from the foundational myth

which gives support and purpose to the total enterprise a congregation loses momentum and direction. Immobility can result with little appreciation of why a sense of meaning has disappeared from shared events.

10. Schleiermacher, Friedrich. *The Christian Faith.* This central principle is fundamental to Schleiermacher's attempt to use an empirical starting point for theology.

11. Niebuhr, H. Richard. op. cit., p.41.

12. Meland, Bernard. *Faith and Culture,* London: George Allen and Unwin, 1955, pp54-55. Used by permission. The sense of depth, a dominant metaphor for Meland is for him 'a genuine dimension of experience beyond conscious experience which, when related to the conscious life, illumines and enhances it in qualitative ways'. (p.35)

13. Martin Buber's remark is apposite, 'I possess nothing but the everyday out of which I am never taken . . . I know no fulness but each mortal hour's fulness of claim and responsibility'. *Between Man and Man,* New York, Macmillan Paperbacks Edition, 1967, p.14. Copyright Routledge & Kegan Paul Ltd. Used by permission.

CHAPTER THREE

A Method of Approach

I N SEEKING TO DEVELOP AN INTERPRETATION OF THE CULTURE of a local congregation the issue of method becomes a major concern. Those who engage in the project through one of the course offerings in religious education within the United Faculty of Theology and the Evangelical Theological Association, Melbourne, are given the following statement on the purpose and goal of the course.

'The task is (1) to seek to understand the meaning(s) system of a local congregation at its inner symbolic depth against six criteria – time, space, language, intimacy, circumstance, consensus; (2) to develop an interpretative grid for ministry to the congregation; (3) to devise, as an outflow of that perspective, creative projects of transformation which give direction and thrust to the life of the congregation.'

OPENINGS FOR MINISTRY

A critical idea central to the design of the project is that of 'openings for ministry'. Implicit in the use of this phrase is the assumption that in the life of any congregation there are opportunities and needs which can be the basis of creative ventures in shared ministry. Conversely, the culture of a congregation is impervious to change in some areas of its life and attempts to bring about transformation in those areas are doomed to failure. To employ a crude image by way of illustration, if you are travelling towards a brick wall at great speed on a motor cycle with the intention of passing beyond the wall it is helpful to know where the openings exist that will enable you to pass through the wall without harm. Many attempts to bring about changes in the life and mission of local congregations have come to an abrupt halt because, by analogy, the attempted changes have been directed at the most solid areas of resistance.

Local cultures change slowly. They become resistant to change if the changes suggested threaten deeply held sentiments of the people. The notion of 'openings for ministry' is not an idea that attempts to ignore conflict nor to deny that any growth or change in group behaviour is painful at some level. It is rather concerned with the art of the possible. It enshrines a reality principle that honours the local congregation as it is, and seeks to transcend the limitations resident there by uncovering openings for ministry. When identified they can be nurtured for the flowering of the congregation's identity and mission.

The strength of this concept and a failure to understand it was revealed in one congregation where a new minister, seeing the financial liability of the congregation, determined to arrest the decline by instituting a planned giving program. Some patient research would have revealed to him that two strong elements in the congregation were against a successful prosecution of his plan. The first was a previous experience with a professional fund-raising group which had split the congregation. Unity was a deeply held value among the people and from the painful conflicts of that first experience the value of unity had become more firmly established. An organised fund-raising campaign, however justified at a rational level, was a symbol of dissension to the people at the affective level of their shared life.

Secondly, within the congregation a firm conviction about the responsibility of the congregation to the needs of the Third World was being implemented by a committee, the major recommendations of which cut against any attempt to raise money for domestic needs, particularly in relation to church property. It was partly a question of timing, partly a question of strategy, but mostly the conflict that ensued was because of strongly-held sentiment about the unity of the congregation. A student in the congregation researching the culture of the people believed that the anatomy of the conflict revealed a lack of understanding of what lay beneath the hostility. He concluded that the attempt to develop the notion of stewardship, through the strategy of a planned giving campaign, was ill advised. There was no present opening for ministry. Only when the past had been successfully negotiated in relation to the dominant norm of congregational unity could change occur.

DESIGN AND LOCATION

All participants in the course are required to spend a year with the congregation they choose to study. Two designs are employed, each with its own strengths and limitations.

In the first case, three students are placed with a minister in one congregation. Each student chooses two of the six criteria (time, space, language, intimacy, circumstance, consensus) and spends ten hours a week for eight months working within the congregation, attempting to identify how the particular criteria find expression in the life of the people.

Each week the students, ministers of the parish, the course organiser and another parish minister, who acts as a process consultant, gather to discuss what has occurred. Regular progress reports from all parties are given. In addition the cluster of four in each parish meets regularly to plan action and to seek interpretation of what is happening. Support related to personal struggle is offered here as well as at seminar meetings. This design has been used in two neighbouring parishes involving six students in all.

The second pattern employed has students working by themselves in a variety of parish locations. Most of the students are fulfilling field education requirements and are under the supervision of the parish minister. Weekly discussions are held on the six criteria in first term. In second term each student meets in a small group of peers similarly engaged in the study of a particular community. There each person gives a weekly presentation using the tools of interpretation provided. These tools make up the substance of Section Three of this book. Not all students are in parishes. Some work within a religious community or order of the Catholic Church, others in schools, some as chaplains in hospitals. Each year locations vary according to the student body, but most spend their time within the context of the local congregation.

The strength of the design lies in exposing students to the actual life of a congregation, thus adding parish experience to that of library, chapel and lecture room as a focus of learning.

In the final phase students develop a plan for ministry in the particular congregation. The plan identifies openings for ministry, indicates how the openings emerge from the analysis and interpretation of the inner life of the congregation, and how they conceive of their projects as transformative.

SOME FINDINGS

The major gain for course participants has not been confined to the development of interpretative skills. It has helped students recognise that the gap between seminary education and the life of the local congregation is great, amounting, in many cases, to the construction of a false reality in seminary which is remote from and unmoved by actual circumstances of parish existence.

This recognition has made it clear to those involved that we often do not know what to look for when we explore the social location of a congregation and the hidden inner reality of its life. A lack of skill in this area has unearthed anxiety about bringing off significant change. The anxiety arises because of a deep-seated threat, not just to role performance, but also to self identity.

The progression of the course usually moves participants to a position where they have a measure of confidence about themselves and their ability to work creatively with a congregation. Curiously, spirits are warmed by the paradoxes uncovered, as if they help explain how much ministry involves learning to address the mystery that lies at the heart of congregational life. As a student wrote: 'Parish ministry is the coming together of two unique dynamics – the parish and the minister. Each must know, appreciate and accept the other. Growth takes place out of the interaction of these two in real meeting and dialogue. This means I cannot impose my expectations on a parish of what it should be, either for me or for the world, but rather let it be what it is, and what it will be.'

To learn to let the parish be what it is remains the first step in the release of originative energies for ministry and service. The second is to call the congregation into that which it can yet be in that fertile encounter between the local situation, its leaders and the people. Behind this recognition is a conviction that the congregation has hope and faith as its creative ground. The struggle is to actualise and possess as communal gift that which is given as promise. Out of that struggle, so we learn, God births in us light and life.

A GUIDE TO BEING THERE

The task as defined is three-fold. The first step is to set about naming the culture of a particular congregation. The second is interpreting what is thereby identified. The third is a process of remaking, directed to using the possibilities for change and growth which have been called 'openings for ministry'.[1]

What has not been discussed is the method of gathering information, which needs to be consistent with the aim of honouring what the congregation is. The most useful of a possible range of methods for gathering data is that method which in the field of cultural anthropology is called participant-observation.[2]

There are several assumptions in the participant-observer model of socio-cultural analysis that are central to its functioning. The first of these is that any analysis not directed and shaped by the symbols of the people being studied is suspect. The interpretation most honoured is the interpretation the people themselves place on what is under question. It is the particular symbolic meanings which are significant to the culture itself which the participant-observer seeks to identify.

The participant-observer gains knowledge by taking on the perspective and style of those being studied, and attempts to recreate in his or her own imagination and experience the thoughts and feelings which are in the minds of the people. It is through a process of symbolic interpretation of the experienced culture that the observer works with the data and discovers meaning in them.

The guidelines in understanding the role of participant-observer include the following:

(1) The participant-observer shares in the activities and sentiments of the people. This involves face-to-face relationships, and direct contact with their shared life.

(2) The role of participant-observer requires both a necessary detachment and personal involvement.

(3) The participant-observer is a normal part of the culture and the life of the people under observation. He or she does not come as an expert, but rather as a learner who, in order to learn, participates in the life of the people.

(4) The role of the participant-observer is consistent within the congregation, so that no confusion is created by unexpected changes of behaviour or alternating of roles.

(5) The participant-observer has as a target a symbolic level of meaning in the life of the congregation which cannot be gained from observing external behaviour alone, as would be the case for a detached observer.

The proper arena of exploration is the imaginative life of the people, their stories, metaphors, allegories, myths, analogies, proverbs and acknowledged paradoxes. To enter in, the participant-observer must understand the personal meaning that central organising symbols have for the people. That is the key to understanding their life. As Blumer says, what is sought is 'a meaningful picture – abetted by apt illustrations which enable one to grasp the reference in terms of one's own experience'.[3]

The insistence on the interpretation being subject to the culture's own self-understanding is to overcome the perceptual bias that all observers bring to an alien community. Niebuhr states the point in the following way. 'The understanding that the spatio-temporal point of view of an observer enters into his knowledge of reality, so that no universal knowledge of things as they are in themselves is possible, so that all knowledge is conditioned by the standpoint of the knower, plays the same rôle in our thinking that the idealistic discoveries of the seventeenth and eighteenth centuries and the evolutionary discovery of the nineteenth played in the thought of earlier generations'.[4] To know and to understand requires participation and an openness to the communication of the culture in its own language and through its own modes of interaction and ritual gestures.

THINKING ABOUT THE CULTURE

The style of thinking appropriate to the participant-observer is not that logical, abstract and rational mode which is more at home in the laboratory and the computer centre. What is required is that mode of encountering reality which Heidegger calls meditative thinking.[5] Meditative thinking is a style of thinking which is synthetic, imaginative, holistic and metaphorical. This mode of thinking, which is characteristic of the right hemisphere of the brain, is no less thinking than that of the analytic mode of thinking, which is located in the left hemisphere of the brain.[6] Meditative thinking seeks by imagination and intuition to grasp the webs of significance that hold the meanings of the people.

The realm of meaning which has its depths in the unconscious and pre-conscious as well as the conscious levels of life is not accessible to the rational. This is largely because the very occurrence of meaning emerges by the juxtaposition of logically incompatible elements. Such is the case in the literary creation of metaphor. Many of the parables Jesus told have a structure of meaning that defy precise logical analysis. The Christian confession of the 'God-Man' is of this kind of thinking. It does not make its meaning accessible by logical analysis, although 'common-sense' may grasp its power.

The style of description that the participant-observer seeks therefore is one of synthesis, not analysis. Most of us who have come through logical, left-hemisphere dominated education systems are not readily able to escape the rationalist orientation which is the product of such systems. It is not possible to capture the beauty of a rose by dissecting the flower. But some of its wonder can be captured by writing a haiku. It is that kind of approach, one of falling under the spell of the mystery of the community, that is appropriate in the pursuit of the inner life of the congregation.

This is not to suggest an anti-rational mode of inquiry. Nor is it, despite the inevitable appearance to the contrary, to lapse into a hopeless romanticism about the life of the congregation. It is to suggest rather that if one seeks the subtle and elusive webs of meaning that bind together the inner life of a community, they will not be captured in the net of analytic thought. The analytic mode is inappropriate to uncovering what is sought.

When such meanings are appropriated by those seeking to understand it involves being open to primal visual images that have their force precisely because they cannot be brought decisively or totally under the control of rational processes of thought. C. S. Lewis states the distinction with characteristic precision. 'I am a rationalist. For me reason is the natural organ of truth; but imagination is the organ of meaning. Imagination, producing new metaphors or revivifying old, is not the cause of truth, but its condition.'[7]

It was the contention of Lewis that the symbolic realm in which meaning resides (and which is also the kingdom of faith)[8] is not rationally but imaginatively understood. Only when concepts have been turned into images do they appear real to the human mind. This suggests a process in which images rising from experience are formed into concepts which are then transmuted back into images in order to communicate their truth. Meaning is therefore an integration of both reason and imagination in which reason is guided not by its own structural logic but that which comes co-operatively from the domain of imagination.

This perspective is shared by Michael Polanyi who gives primacy to the creative imagination in the sciences as well as the arts. He writes that man lives in the meanings he is able to discern.[9] For Polanyi, the meanings which guide us are created when that which is of focal interest is fused with a subsidiary level of awareness. He refers to this as the tacit dimension. Meaning comes into being when a movement occurs from the tacit dimension to the focal or observed object of awareness, and in the integration personal knowledge occurs. The creative imagination is that capacity of the human which effects the integration of the parts into a coherent whole, and thereby calls into being new possibilities of thought and action. For Polanyi therefore the creative imagination is a revolutionary capacity of the human mind, which upon the basis of intuition leaps to a resolution of a problem. This may subsequently be sustained by experimentation and demonstration.[10]

Moving from within the same viewpoint Paul Ricoeur sees the symbol as that which both calls into being and unveils the sub-strata of meaning in human experience.[11] 'Man's ultimate concern must be expressed symbolically, because symbolic language alone is able to express the ultimate.'[12] In these words Paul Tillich reinforces what has been claimed by Lewis, Polanyi and Ricoeur. To be open to the appearing of meaning and the faith that sustains it, it is necessary to abandon a blind trust in objectivity, and to seek a critical receptivity in which one learns to understand by 'sitting where they sit'. An appreciation of a particular ecology of spirit is to be found in the first instance not in analytic processes of the mind but in that less secure realm of the mythopoeic.

PROBLEMS AND TENSIONS OF THE MARGINAL COMMUNICANT

There is a danger in the participant-observer method of understanding a culture which parallels that of a tight-rope walker. As Gwen Neville writes, 'They (anthropologists) risk the constant danger of either falling into the chasm of subjectivity that is feared by all scientists or of becoming caught immobilized by the conflicts of attempting to be objective about their own cultural meanings, values, and beliefs'.[13]

This danger is acute where understanding a congregation puts at risk the professional status and emotional security of the minister. Within the experience of five years working on the project of understanding the culture of a local congregation, many participants have been plunged into crisis about their view of themselves and the role they are preparing to undertake. Seeing a congregation as it is can be demoralising for some, and to be asked to leave the security of an objective disengaged position threatening to others. The risk cannot be taken away.

A further source of tension is the reliance upon others implicit in the method. The orientation and perceptual bias of the newcomer can significantly distort what is experienced unless it is subject to the control and interpretation of others who indwell the culture in a way the newcomer does not. Most clergy however have not been trained to work co-operatively. Others by inclination choose an individual model as their preferred style of ministry. If one is dependent upon the people to learn the secret of their shared life, the outcome places in jeopardy ideas of authority which rest on doctrines of a revealed word uniquely given to a chosen leader. We shape all knowledge by the way we know it. It is necessary to abandon many assumptions about role, status and authority to truly seek to be with and to listen to the people.

Again this movement is a two-edged sword. The longer one is involved with a congregation, and the deeper and richer observations become, the more completely the participant-observer lives in and identifies with the situation. This can lead to a false confidence that the whole is known. Yet what any individual sees, however sensitive and informed, is not only part of a mysterious whole but only one perception of that whole. A principle of uncertainty needs to be invoked to protect the participant-observer from too much assurance about what can never be understood completely. As time and circumstances change, so do the perceptions of participants.

That is why the exploration of the life of the people needs to be undertaken co-operatively, with colleagues and other members of the congregation who live inside the experience of the people. The method requires a view sufficiently removed to examine the culture with a measure of objectivity, and a commitment compassionate enough to strive to help the congregation become more completely itself. The term of Gwen Neville is a felicitous one. The stance is that of a 'marginal communicant' [14] at least when the task of participant-observer is being undertaken.

'PASSING OVER' AND CONFESSIONAL THEOLOGY

John Dunne, the Catholic author, offers a similar approach which he describes as the process of 'passing over'[15] from the viewpoint of the observer into the world of the other(s) one seeks to know by imaginative identification with the other and his or her world. In so doing Dunne argues we can arrive at an understanding of that truth which shapes the vision of the person and that person's life world. The person who passes over is then able to return to his own perspective, which, through a process of sympathetic understanding, can be enriched by transforming the truth seized imaginatively 'over there' into one's own perspective.

As Dunne describes it, 'When I pass over from my standpoint to that of another, I go not only from my subjective view of myself to his objective view of me, but also from my objective view of him to his subjective view of himself. So when I come to realize that there is no absolute standpoint for me, I realize too that there is no absolute standpoint for him'.[16]

The gain of such a method of passing over in imagination to another world is that two essential ingredients of community, participation and communicability, intrinsic to the process of understanding, are present and honoured by the way of approach.

The intention of the method used in the case of appreciating the life of the congregation is to do more than simply understand. It is to give shape and substance to what Niebuhr describes as confessional theology.

'. . . Its home is the church; its language is the language of the church; and with the church it is directed toward the universal from which the church knows itself to derive its being and to which it points in all its faith and works.'[17] Such a confessional theology is derived not in isolation from but by response to, the Holy in the believing experience of the congregation.

In order to pass over intelligently it is necessary to identify structural components which will serve as a guide in the process of 'naming the culture'. These dimensions have already been identified as time, space, language, intimacy, circumstance and consensus. It is to the investigation of these ideas that we now turn our attention.

NOTES TO CHAPTER 3

1. The words 'change' and 'growth' can be understood as representing different and mutually exclusive processes. The intention in using both words is to underline that transformation can occur in continuity with present patterns – an organic metaphor such as growth – or in discontinuity with accepted practice – a disjunctive metaphor such as change in a radical form. In both cases re-education of some kind is involved.

2. Those interested in a more comprehensive treatment of the role of the participant-observer should consult such sources as: Alderfer, C.P. and Brown, L.D. *Learning from Changing: Organisational Diagnosis and Development*, Beverly Hills, California: Sage Productions, 1975; Bentzen, M.M. et al. *Changing Schools: The Magic Feather Principle*, New York: McGraw Hill, 1974; Cameron, W.G. *Toward Dynamic Equilibrium: An Inservice Approach to Organisation Development*, Sydney: Division of Services, Inservice Education, N.S.W. Department of Education, 1978; Bruhn, Severyn. *The Human Perspective in Sociology*, Englewood Cliffs, N.S.: Prentice Hall Inc., 1966.

3. Blumer, Herbert. 'What is Wrong With Social Theory', *American Sociological Review*, Vol. 19 (Feb. 1954).

4. Niebuhr, op. cit. p.5.

5. See Heidegger, Martin. *Discourse on Thinking*, translated by John M. Anderson and E. Hans Freund, New York: Harper and Row, 1959. Referring to meditative thinking, John Anderson in his introduction, remarks, 'We might think of it, metaphorically, as the activity of walking along a path which leads to Being' (p.25), which is supported by his earlier observation, 'Meditative thinking is thinking which is open to its content, open to what is given' (p.24).

6. The volume *The Nature of Human Consciousness* (ed. Robert E. Ornstein), New York: The Viking Press, Inc., 1974, is a useful reference point to a field of inquiry which is growing rapidly.

7. Lewis, C.S. 'Bluspels and Flalansferes' in *Rehabilitations*, London: Oxford Press, 1939, p.158. Reproduced by permission of Curtis Brown Ltd., London, on behalf of C.S. Lewis Pte. Ltd. Corbin Carnell in *Bright Shadow of Reality:C.S. Lewis and the Feeling Intellect*, Grand Rapids, Michigan: William B. Eerdmans Publishing Company, 1974, comments on Lewis in the following way: 'For Lewis as for Charles Williams there can be no clear-cut separation between

flesh and spirit, between the natural and the supernatural. They exist in a kind of broken, paradoxical unity. In man's nature animal and spirit "co-inhere" in such a way that we laugh about our animal functions and yet regard the disembodied spirit (or ghost) with fear.' (See footnote 3, pp100-101.) It is the nature of the given which pleads for an incarnated method of seeing for the spirit through the flesh of the body corporate.

The notion of 'sehnsucht', the feeling intellect, so important for Lewis, is not significantly different from the idea of meditative thinking in Heidegger.

8. 'For there is no substitute for the use of symbols and myths: they are the language of faith.' Lewis, op cit, p.51. A similar viewpoint is held by Paul Tillich: 'The language of faith is the language of symbols.' Tillich, Paul. *The Dynamics of Faith*, London: George Allen and Unwin Ltd., 1957, p.45. By permission of Harper & Row, Publishers, Inc.

9. Polanyi, Michael and Prosch, Harry. *Meaning*, Chicago: University of Chicago Press, 1975.

10. This position of Polanyi is argued extensively in *Personal Knowledge: Towards a Post Critical Philosphy*, Chicago: University of Chicago Press, 1958.

11. Ricoeur, Paul. *The Symbolism of Evil*, translated by Emerson Buchanan, New York: Beacon Paperback, 1969, pp10-18.

12. Tillich, op cit, p.41.

13. Neville and Westerhoff, op cit, p.71.

14. ibid, p.75 ff.

15. Dunne, John S. *A Search for God in Time and Memory*, Notre Dame, Indiana: University of Notre Dame Press, 1977. Also *The Way of All the Earth*, New York: The Macmillan Company, 1972, p.6.

16. Dunne, John S. *The Way of All the Earth*, New York: The Macmillan Company, 1972, p.6.

17. Niebuhr, op. cit., p.21.

PART TWO
NAMING

CHAPTER FOUR

Time and Space

W*HAT IS THE PREDOMINANT SENSE OF TIME IN THE congregation? To what events and rituals is it most immediately linked? What are the sacred locations? On significant occasions, what is confessed in relationship to such locations?*

The task, which has been conceived against the broad question of what forms, shapes and sustains a faith community, is to learn to see what is present in a congregation in fresh and open ways, to interpret what is revealed through a coherent framework, and thus to identify openings for ministry. These openings for ministry guide the process of educating a people of God by a sympathetic transformation of the ethos which directs congregational sociality.

The first step, called here 'naming', is to view the congregation through the central organising concepts of time, space, language, intimacy, circumstance and consensus.[1] These concepts are held to be essential forming dimensions of any community. As a total picture of the congregation is built up, these dimensions can be employed as the skeleton upon which characteristic and discernible clusters of congregational concerns are built. Just as in some fishing nets large knots hold the net together, so, as a picture of the people's life is assembled, these central organising concepts give strength to the revealed pattern. To change the image, if an X-ray could be taken of the congregation, its supporting structure would be revealed as a symbiotic union of the six foundational dimensions.

In employing these six categories, the intention is to learn how they function to give shape to congregational life. Understanding that unique configuration is what is involved in the process of naming.

TIME

It is not a simple matter to separate time from space for each interpenetrates the other. Henri Bergson argued that time was always built on a space model. If you look at a wrist-watch you immediately see that the device of the clock converts time to spatial units, seconds, minutes, hours. Similarly a calendar transforms time into units of days, weeks, months, years.[2]

Time is not from this perspective an intuition of unbroken presentness as in Aboriginal society, but a one dimensional reality of successive events. The device of the clock and the calendar illustrate how western culture has structured time to serve its purposes. There is nothing intrinsic in nature itself which compels particular societies to reckon time in terms of units such as days, weeks or seasons. The Western passion for reckoning time accurately and consistently indicates that we experience time as a social reality. Calendar time is social time.

> '. . . the time that is in man is not abstract but particular and concrete;
> it is not a general category of time but rather the time of a definite society
> with distinct language, economic and political relations, religious faith
> and social organization.'[3]

Clearly different cultures have varying time perspectives. An English clock 'runs'. A Spanish clock 'walks'. The urgency for action that resides in the breast of a Western volunteer dominated by a certain concept of time does not find an echo in the social expectations of the African village where he hopes to get things done. Transcorporation time pays obeisance to the stop-watch that turns units of time into economic value. The farmer grazing his cattle on the coastal plains has little or no sense of time as drenched with commercial virtue. Time is 'wasted', 'killed' and 'exhausted' in one culture and 'renewed', 'danced' and 'swallowed' in another. Time is in us and we are in time in ways appropriate to our cultural expectations. Time is socially experienced time.

INSTITUTIONAL AND COMMUNITY TIME

Time is encountered in two ways in our social experience. The first is objective time or institutional time. Time in this sense is spatialised by our social constructions and is capable of conceptualisation as a particular entity we can react to with claims and demands.

Community time by contrast is existential and personal. It has its force not in external social construction but in subjective communal processes that can be experienced as 'timeless'. What gives significance to this second stream of awareness in time is its relative freedom from the prison of chronology. The past can live in the present, the present in the past, and both in the future. The mystery of our time sense in community time is to recognise that it is infused with an 'otherness', even that it is in Plato's phrase the 'changing image of eternity'.

Niebuhr states it well. 'What is past is not gone; it abides in us as our memory; what is future is not non-existent but present in us as our potentiality. Time here is organic or it is social, so that past and future associate with each other in the present. Time in our history is not another dimension of the external space world in which we live, but a dimension of our life and our community's being. We are not in this time but it is in us. It is not associated with space in a unity of space-time but it is inseparable from life in the continuity of life-time . . . Such time is not a number but a living, a stream of consciousness, a flow of feeling, thought and will.'[4]

In focusing attention on the category of time five separate designations can be used. These are past time present, present time present, future time present, above time present, below time present. The word time in each case refers not to institutional but to community time, or that inner time sense referred to as existential time.

1. *Past time present*

The act of remembering is essential for the creation of identity and corporate integrity in any community. A community is by definition a sharing together of significant happenings, the substance of which comes largely from remembering. When stories are told we re-member the memories of others and make them our own. A Christian community re-members the story of Jesus in such a way that its present life is made healthy by that curative process of memory. As John Knox puts it, 'To share in a common memory is to participate in an experience of the meaning of a past event whose actuality can be as little doubted as the meaning itself'.[5]

This memory which is 'inner memory' is not always accurate. The case of the killing of Goliath by David is a case in point.[6] Its power lies rather in preserving something of the concrete quality, the intentional impact and the felt meaning of an event in the past. What is described as inner memory lies buried in the structure of a people's experience. Sometimes generative possibilities exist in a community's life as frozen memories, which can be freed to work their recreative magic again. The critical factor in the sense of past time present is the nature of the memories themselves 'and, as far as inner existence is concerned, it is the uniqueness of its memories which more than any other factor distinguishes one community from another'.[7]

An illustration may serve to underline this statement of Knox. In the church building I currently attend for worship there is a visitors book. The book rests on a table inside the church against the back wall. Above the visitors book, fastened to the wall, is a glass case within which rests a large memorial book. Above the glass case there is a clock.

Each Sunday during the year a page in the book is turned, and the visitor who stoops to write his or her name in the visitors book can see beneath the glass the names, written in a shaky spidery hand, of those who have lived and died in the faith from this community. I have never found out who turns the pages of the memorial book but when the configuration of clock, memorial diary and visitors book are held together they constitute a cherishing of the congregation's past so powerfully present now that I have no desire to ask who does the turning. It is enough to meditate upon what is confessed in this symbolic unity of past present.

2. *Present time present*

The time sense that indwells a congregation can be negative as well as positive. When we talk of a church being behind the times (anachronistic) what we usually mean is that it does not address current needs to a significant degree. Attempts to give a contemporary air to worship, however, usually have little connection with the past present in congregational experience and appear disjointed and alien to congregational sentiment as a result.

Yet the colloquial sense of 'now time' refers to a consciousness in which past present fits with and enriches contemporary experience. Augustine argued that intuition was the appropriate form of engagement in present time. The intuition of which he spoke was not confined to a single moment but rather, looking backward and forward, named God's present action in the midst of the people.

The discerning of the signs of the times therefore is not to be confused with making visible the fashions and styles of modernity. It has to do with addressing the present moment in a unity of consciousness that sees life and action responding to the needs of the hour. The move to unite the Presbyterians, Methodists and Congregationalists into the Uniting Church in Australia, which was effected in 1976, was an occasion for many congregations in which the present called for decision both in continuity and discontinuity with past traditions.

A comment on one situation by a student indicates how the present can be fumbled by a lack of awareness of what is involved in responding in the present to a new self-understanding.

'There is not the same willingness to share in the history of the development and growth of the new joint Methodist-Presbyterian community. This may be due to the fact that both the former congregations were not given an opportunity to share in a common experience when they came together; and therefore they tend to share significant events of the past but separate congregations. There does not seem to have been any major, special symbolic occasion when all of the present members entered into a new community, shared a common history and interests as a people of God.'

Another story of the same kind is that of a congregation who sold their church building and moved to join with a sister congregation. No one suggested they bring symbols from their former sanctuary with them. So they grieved in their new environment for signs that honoured their past story and proclaimed that here they belonged.

By contrast, in one congregation where I was present on the fourth anniversary of the Uniting Church, three candles lit the one large candle in the sanctuary. Then each member of the congregation was given a square chocolate-coated biscuit. The first corner was bitten off and as it was savoured, memories of life in the former Presbyterian dispensation were invited. The next corner was bitten off and Methodist history was remembered; the next the Congregational heritage, and the last, our present experience in the Uniting Church. What was left was a cross. As one body we consumed the remaining portion of our biscuit, thus taking into ourselves that symbol of Christ which bound us now in a new life in him. It was both past time present and present time present in a celebrative unity.

3. *Future time present*

If synchrony characterises present time present, a synchronising that integrates dimensions of time in present awareness, then the future dimension in present time anticipates a fulfilment of what is hoped for in contemporary experience. As memory and intuition mark the sense of past and present, expectation infuses the dimension of the future in the present. It is resident most powerfully in the potentiality which lies within congregational living.

What calls forth that potentiality is a vision in which alienation is overcome by a commitment to a freely chosen future. So persuasive is its promise that the congregation asserts its force and is bound by its appeal. The images which define the anticipated future have their source in biblical narrative, the tap root of which is the promise that Jesus offered about the kingdom of God present in him. Such images, in a contemporary location, include those of a pilgrim people, the coming kingdom of God's action, the new creation which makes all things whole, a new heaven and a new earth. God is bringing into being a people obedient to his will who will learn through their struggle together who God is, and who they are as a consequence.

In many local congregations founding events can be uncovered, an originating vision defined. Sometimes that vision comes out of the death of the secure and familiar. Sometimes it is a choice to seek a new path. Always what is sought is anticipated with hope. The history of the move to union in the Uniting Church is a story of local congregations dying to their separate identity in order that a new destiny might be wrought. Without that vision of God's call to go out not knowing what would befall, prudential reasons for union would never have carried the day. Without anticipation and hope, without vision the people perish. Future time in the present is as necessary as any other dimension of time to the shared faith of the whole community.

4. *Above time present*

The presence of the transcendent in the life of a community can be understood to make its appearance in both negative and positive ways. In its negative form the life of the people is an escape from the reality of personal and community reality. The people live into visions of a reality to come, fantastic in its benefits, and by implication despising all that is currently experienced.

So other-wordly is the vision of the people that they leap above daily experience by a projection of themselves into an apocalyptic future. The denial this represents of life in the present plane of existence means that a false reality has been constructed, an analog of the schizophrenic who lives in a world little related to the world of other people.

Students have been introduced to congregations where charismatic or fundamentalist elements have refused all traffic with the present commerce of church and society. The possibility of serving such a parish has seemed beyond their imagination and skill. Can the dimension of transcendence be grounded positively by returning the people to their own story? The seeking of God's saving action exclusively in the future usually involves a denial of God's action in the past and present.

It is easy to dismiss such communities as pathological, as many have done with the Jones community in South America that destroyed itself in obedience to his command. Yet such elements are present in many churches, exerting a demonic influence. Rejection of the present can spawn a progeny determined to escape into a 'timeless order'.

5. *Below time present*

The case of below time present is the opposite of above time present. 'When I first visited the congregation I noticed that the past was referred to in every conversation . . . I was given the impression that church members looked back to a "golden era" in the past when the church was at its greatest vitality. . .'

'The internal structure of the community, its thought patterns, group dynamics and methods of communication are, I feel, more suited to a past society than a present one. Consequently it is not surprising to see that the status of members appeared to be connected to their past.'[8]

In the case of the congregation written about above it was a general consensus that 'we are a dying church'. That judgment was not communicated in a spirit of determination to fight but rather one of resignation. 'Time' had passed them by. They conceded 'time' hung heavily on their hands. Time was only past time. The image was that of a people submerged in time, drowning with no expectation of helping themselves or being helped.

A culture of this kind suffers from a poverty of the spirit in which hope has fled and energy for renewal cannot be summoned to fight what is generally agreed to be inevitable. Ministering to rural communities which are dying, or urban congregations trapped by population shifts and the problem of an ageing constituency can be difficult precisely because the dominant time sense is that of below time present. A recognition of this dimension of time can lead to an arrest of that feeling of falling behind the times. Because time is socially experienced it can be recognised that what is seen as inevitable had been chosen by the congregation to be inevitable. At one congregational meeting that plotted the future of a congregation's life to a level below survival possibilities in five to ten years, I was accosted in the aisle by an eighty-two year old lady waving her walking stick. 'What are we going to do,' she said, 'we can't take this decline without a fight!' A spirited response in the proper sense of spirit-filled and one which, despite the gravity of the situation, was not intimidated by the crushing weight of the present. In such cases the spirit is victor over time and its inclination of tyranny.

It is because our experience of time is disclosed in public language that exploring it in the ways suggested can help locate the congregation in relation to the kairos of the present hour.

SPACE

Space, like time, is a fundamental category that defines human existence. Further, as Cassirer remarks, 'There is no achievement or creation of the spirit which is not in some way related to the world of space and which does not in a sense seek to make itself at home in it'.[9] Space is capable of bearing all of those properties we ascribe to the human. It can be warm or cold, open or closed, light or dark, welcoming or menacing and so on.

Space can be impersonal and personal. A graphic illustration of this difference strikes the traveller to Delhi. New Delhi was created by the British when they controlled India. Characterised by broad roads and impressive buildings the major bureaucratic agencies are located in this architecturally contrived area. Delhi by contrast is chaotic, teeming with life. It has an organic connectedness in the very patterning of its buildings and roads. Order is the dominant motif of the one, intimate disorder that of the other. Objectivity is written into the design of New Delhi; subjectivity, by its very absence of intentionality, imprinted on Delhi. The boundary between one and the other is discernible. It is a threshold of meaning.

The threshold, in relation to this idea of space, takes on profound significance. When we cross a threshold our experience of reality can change. We know ourselves to be invited into a different plane of existence. Entering the door of our house is one such threshold which takes us into what the French philosopher Gaston Bachelard called 'felicitous space'. '... the human value of the sorts of space that may be grasped, that may be defended against adverse forces, the space we love.'[10] In this sense, following Bachelard, all inhabited space, space that is lived in, has the essence of the nature of home. It is not without significance that the church building is referred to as the 'house' of God, nor that there one can find 'sanctuary'. Where a people travel the tabernacle becomes the centre 'home'. When a people become settled the house becomes home and both are a large cradle fashioned to give nurturing dimension to a particular area of space. There is a territorial imperative in all creatures, and for humans space is the medium in which spiritual productivity first establishes itself.

CATEGORIES OF SPACE: SACRED AND SECULAR

The word religion comes from the root *relegere* meaning to be careful. Religious observance is directed to confining the dimension of the sacred to certain times and places when it can be approached in safety. The frightful lightning in the sky can be used to boil a kettle in the home if domesticated with care.

The impulse of religion therefore derives from a recognition that interwoven in space is a basic opposition of sacred and profane dimensions. Space can bear the quality of sacred and secular substance. It can be trivialised by human artifact or, in the case of cathedral or temple, it can constitute, by its opposition to the secular, 'the unique mythical atmosphere in which it stands – the magical aura that surrounds it'.[11]

There is always a threshold in space that we seek to control, and yet we cross it unwittingly sometimes because we do not know it is there. Objective space, whose dimension is secular, even trivial, can in a moment become intuitive space filled with a numinous presence. It is theology that seeks to *place* us in relation to our world and to alert us to the dimension of ultimacy that pervades all of human experience. Space then is a category of experience.

SPACE AS A COMMUNICATION SYSTEM

It follows that when we order space it communicates, in the very design, our view of what is important and what is not. To discern the value ascribed to spatial reality by a congregation, and to appreciate the symbols that are cherished by the people, is a way of moving closer to the centre of their shared life.

The sacred space of the congregation is not only in the sanctuary. It can include the graveyard beside the church, or a particular pew where a great and revered leader sat. Occasionally it can be the Sunday school hall, a memorial garden, or a splintered cross in the grounds to which pilgrimage is made once a year on Good Friday.

Before turning to categories of space as guides to our quest of appreciating the idea of space, it is necessary to identify three elements in sacred space that exist within its dynamic. These elements are (1) security which is the desire for peace,

61

(2) confrontation which constitutes challenge, (3) centredness which affirms unity. As the guide to exploring space is used, the elements of peace, confrontation and unity are found in juxtaposition with each other. The threshold is within our encounter with the Divine. Paradoxically we can be most at peace where it is most dangerous. The relationship is always an ambiguous one.

It can be seen that space takes on dimensions of personality for us and can be filled with 'human' emotions. The space outside the headmaster's office is menacing. The dentist's waiting room can be charged with terror; the magistrates court intimidating; the cathedral ceiling awesome; the cubby in the backyard friendly. One possible pattern for exploring the idea of space is to take the human senses as a guide and explore the congregation's meaningful indwelling of its space through that grid.

The categories thus available are (1) auditory, (2) visual, (3) sensory. Included in the latter are touch, taste, and smell. What then does the way the people indwell their space tell us about the 'deepest down things' that claim their allegiance?

1. *Auditory space*

To enter a church building of the Reformed tradition, with the pulpit located in the centre, is to know that auditory space is controlled by the spoken word in that tradition. The status of the word as preached dictates interior design, testifies to an understanding of the role of scripture, the nature of authority, and the mission of the church. Implicit in the very control of auditory space are assumptions about the way God communicates with the people.

By contrast, a Quaker gathering does not fill space with sound, but listens to that inner space which a waiting silence testifies is unlimited. Sound-less space which is filled with 'that nothing which is not nothing' is more awe-full in the tradition of the Friends because it testifies to what is believed, the efficacy of the light of Christ within and its guiding virtue.

Musicians live predominantly in auditory space which is coloured by the sounds of chants and harmonies. It is more likely therefore, in a rich diverse liturgical tradition, that music claims as much attention in the enactment of the liturgy as the sermon. That very emphasis can indicate the role of the believer as that of an observer of the sacred ritual, and its proper rehearsal. In the case of the Methodist tradition, the emphasis on the hymn as celebration of personal experience, the very soil from which the Methodist movement grew, is an efficacious sign both of the inner experience of the worshipper and his or her present participation in the spirit-filled life. The Salvation Army has its particular pattern of music, as well as the penitents form which by its presence testifies to what is believed and confessed about God's dealings with us, the one directly related to the other.

A Catholic nun, who as part of her project attended a parish in the Reformed Calvinistic tradition, came away with the conclusion that she had been confronted with 'cerebral challenge, not communal reality', the latter being her own tradition. One curious story about the control of auditory space came from a situation where members of a church choir had built the pipe organ used for worship. The student discovered that the use of the organ in worship took priority over everything else. The status of the choir was equally elevated. It did not matter what was played on the organ, just so long as the organ played and the choir sang.

The sound of bells, the clash of money emptied, sung liturgies, silence, organ, guitar, all of these fill the meaning space of the people. Careful attention to auditory space can lead to the seminal understandings that guide the people. The carillon that rings out its message from the church tower declares all space sacred. The angelus fills each day with the presence of the Divine.

2. *Visual space*

The dramatic impact made by high altars in certain cathedrals is testimony of the communicative power of symbols and the fashioning of sacred space to reflect the grandeur of God. It is possible to gain a measure of understanding of the sustaining myth of the people by travelling up the steps which ascend to the separated space where a candle flicker signifies the presence of the reserve host.

When, by contrast, a church building has its altar or communion table in the centre of the assembly there is a clear message about God's presence. Murals, banners, colourful pulpit falls, baptismal font, flags, lectern, pulpit, vestments, location of pews, open areas; all of these can speak of what the people confess in common.

So too can the dedication plaques, the memorial centres and relics or artifacts. There is a story told of the attempt to discover the most popular exhibit of the Museum of Science and Industry in Chicago. A conclusion was reached by measuring the wear of the tiles around exhibits. Because of the regular need to renew floor tiles around the chicken hatching display it was concluded that here was the major focus of attention for visitors.

In small churches the care of brass fittings, the renewal of flowers and their location, the preferred meeting places for talk, the avoidance of certain areas, a genuflection, can communicate significant data. Vestries can tell a story. In some the portraits or photographs of past clergy are arrayed; in others the original architectural plans for the then new church. There are places for public and private devotion.

In all of this, including the placing of the central symbols of the community, much can be discerned. One student identified the ambiguous acceptance of the Uniting Church in one parish, formerly Methodist, when he saw that the symbol of the Uniting Church was placed behind the choir. It was hanging crookedly on the wall, as yet not a part of the people's identity, nor within their focused care. At another congregation students were greeted with, 'I suppose you'll want to sit in your normal place'. As a student noted in his diary, 'we were assigned a "normal place" even though this was only our second Sunday in the parish'. The social structure of the congregation, it was discovered through this clue, was patterned by spatial preference, according to years of affiliation with the congregation.

Two other illustrations will suffice. When leaving the church building members of a congregation were funnelled through a single door so that the minister could greet all those at worship as they left. He had developed a practice of setting up appointments for the next week at the door, even to filling his diary. The exodus from church was very slow, the chance of people greeting each other minimised by being kept waiting in the aisle. In this action alone many elements of how authority was exercised in the congregation were evident.

A vase of flowers resting in the baptismal font spoke of the distance of one people from their own story. The investigation of visual space has helped students explain prohibitions on moving around during worship, the pressure to maintain customs by preserving present locations and existing arrangements of church furniture, even to decisions in the board of management.

3. *Sensory space*

The only angel with a sunburnt nose that I have seen is located in the Episcopalian Church at colonial Williamsburg in the state of Virginia. Constant visitors have stroked the bronze figure so that whereas the rest of the angel is dull, the nose gleams brightly in the light. Hardly a definitive liturgical gesture but one illustrative of our need and desire to touch. The tactile dimension of space is everywhere present. Fingers can be dipped in holy water, or seek assurance from the telling of the rosary. Candles can be lit, the feet of saints stroked, the holy book kissed.

In some traditions feet are washed during the Easter season. The peace is passed by the clasping of hands, an embrace or a kiss. The prayer book or Sunday bulletin can itself be a symbol of reassurance as can be the turning of pages to follow the lessons of the day in the Bible. Just as children seek assurance by climbing into a parent's lap so do we in our worship seek the comforting assurance of touch, none more so than in the very substantiality of bread and wine, or the laying on of hands in confirmation or ordination and the flow of water in baptism.

Those we feel closest to we touch the most. In a congregation the level of intimacy and the closeness of that intimacy to the centres of meaning can sometimes be grasped by observing what is touched with reverence.

Similarly the sense of taste. John Westerhoff remarks that eating together is the first response of community. In the church that practice occurs formally in the eucharist but informally in the ubiquitous pot luck suppers or their equivalents in hundreds of parishes in the land. Perhaps that is why the besetting temptation of the ordained minister or priest is gluttony. As the symbol of community he or she is expected tangibly to embody it!

The fragrance of incense for some communities is evocative of the ineffable. Even the perfume of flowers or the studied mustiness of old buildings can be the occasion of moving the spirit to devotion. Along with the senses of touch and taste, the sense of smell can give poignancy to the act of worship that is available in no other way. In one church of my acquaintance an adjoining duck-yard offered its own unique contribution to worship, although the chances of that particular aroma becoming embraced by the church in general is slight. It was nonetheless a far from mute testimony to reality!

Any human experience that is to be communicated to others and preserved in the continuing life of a people must be expressed in symbols. A local congregation lives into its present by taking a particular stance towards its own symbols and that to which they testify. Those symbols can be as diverse as the slave gallery in a church in the south of America or convict pews on the island of Tasmania. It can include the bones of a saint or a jewelled chalice. In some churches the absence of symbols proclaims by the emptiness of space what is believed and loved.

The category of space, when employed in dialogue with the people, can uncover a thousand secrets. The institutionalised order and organised arrangements people give to their way of being together is capable of telling the hidden tale of their spiritual pilgrimage. There are many possible ways of exploring its mystery. Our concern has paralleled that of Cassirer. 'The question of what space signifies for the constitution of the world of things is transformed into another profounder question: what does it signify and accomplish for the building and attainment of specifically spiritual reality?'[12]

NOTES TO CHAPTER 4

1. These six dimensions as fundamental concepts of community were first drawn to my attention in Severyn Bruhn's book *The Human Perspective in Sociology.* They are used here, however, in ways not consistent with Bruhn in either philosophical or functional terms. *The Human Perspective in Sociology,* Englewood Cliffs, N.S.: Prentice Hall Inc., 1966.

2. Something of the force of this observation can be felt when a digital watch is substituted for the more customary clock-face watch. The print-out refers only to the time in the present. It is not possible by reading the numbers to get a sense of time past, or time to come. Changes in technology subtly alter our psychological feel for time, as this minor observation illustrates.

3. Niebuhr, op. cit., p.13.

4. ibid, p.69.

5. Knox, John. *The Church and the Reality of Christ,* New York: Harper and Row, 1962, p.43.

6. There is internal evidence in the Bible that Goliath was killed by one of David's lieutenants. The feat, as was common practice, was ascribed to the leader, David, and a legend developed around the deed that embodied the confession of God's providence in history caring for his people.

7. Knox, op. cit., p.40.

8. Comments of a student on the conversations encountered in his field study for Religious Education.

9. From *Phenomenology of Knowledge,* Vol. 3 (1958), New Haven: Yale University Press, p.150, 'The Philosophy of Symbolic Forms' by Ernst Cassirer. Used by permission.

10. From *The Poetics of Space* (p.xxxi) by Gaston Bachelard, translated by Maria Jolas. Copyright© 1958 by Presses Universitaires de France. Translation Copyright© 1964 by Orion Press, Inc. Reprinted by permission of Viking Penguin Ltd.

11. Cassirer, loc. cit.,

12. Cassirer, op. cit., p.143.

CHAPTER FIVE

Language and Intimacy

W HAT ARE THE KEY WORDS AND PHRASES USED BY THE PEOPLE TO *describe their life together? What are the dominant images shaping congregational life? How is intimacy expressed in the life of the congregation? For what and in what is it focused?*

The dimensions of time and space have their weight for us because of the interpreting influence of our cultural environment. What mediates the sense of personal identity and communal destiny associated with time and space is language and the associated dimension of intimacy. It is not to be concluded that there is an unbroken correlation between language and culture, but the two stand in direct relationship with each other. Perhaps language is the poetics of meaning, as has been claimed. Within human experience it remains the most powerful instrument of self-consciousness, and in any community its influence is persuasive. Language relates essentially to the quest of meaning. As Ricoeur observes, language is the light of the emotions.

LANGUAGE

The importance of language can hardly be overstated. 'All of life hangs on the thin thread of conversation', according to Peter Berger. Heidegger could state, 'language is the house of being'. 'Language makes thinking possible', says Polanyi. Such estimates of the grandeur of language are legion.

The effect of language on our encounter with reality is equally exalted. 'It is quite an illusion to imagine that one adjusts to reality essentially without the use of language and that language is merely an incidental means of solving specific problems of communication and reflection. The fact of the matter is that the "real world" is to a large extent unconsciously built up on the language habits of the group'.[1] Languages, according to Whorl, embody integrated fashions of speaking or background linguistic systems consisting of prescribed modes of expressing thought and experience. The language we learn provides us with a conceptual system for organising experience and a distinctive world view concerning the universe and our relationship to it. The nature of the universe, it follows, is a function of the language in which it is stated. Lichtenberg supports this conclusion. 'Our false philosophy is incorporated in our whole language; we cannot reason without, so to speak, reasoning wrongly. We overlook the fact that speaking, no matter of what, is itself a philosophy.'[2]

LANGUAGE AND THE CHURCH

The church is, like other communities, a community of language. To belong to a faith community it is necessary to learn its unique language and symbolic modes so that the meaning contained therein can be appropriated. The sources of language are many. The Scriptures provide a primary source of the language of the church, as do other traditional writings and prayer books. Traditions and liturgies fused in the worshipping pattern of the congregation also give rise to the language of the faith. Present experience, and the interpretation of that experience christianly, is part of this total pattern. When these sources are brought together a rich tapestry of linguistic and symbolic forms is created.

However, each particular congregation, depending on tradition, local practice, circumstances and preference, usually reveals a selective attitude to the wide range of interpretive images available. That choice is at once a ground of possibility and a limitation for the life of the congregation. As Meland puts it:

'The vocabulary of a cultural group within a given period tends to form afresh around a certain set of experiences which have had decisive or dramatic consequences. In juxtaposition with these innovating terms, and somewhat related to them, one finds a cluster of words and phrases carrying into the period inherited meanings; these words and phrases simultaneously define and restrict the import of experiences which are being freshly described and reported.'[3]

It is useful, as Meland indicates, to recognise that the thinking of the congregation 'moves within its own circumscribing imagery that both illumines the meaning of terms and limits the range of terms which can be used meaningfully'.[4] In order for the language to make sense and the meaning to be communicated, the intelligible discourse of a congregation, as it seeks to celebrate its shared meaning, has of necessity to be in an organic relationship with the life of the congregation or with experiences available to the people. Against this background, possible ways of understanding the language of the congregation can be pursued with profit.

OUTER AND INNER SPEECH

The distinction between outer and inner speech is a broad distinction within which further designations can and should be made. Outer speech is used here to refer to language which is largely descriptive, technical or denotive. It has a measure of objectivity implicit in its use and can be detected in formal and colloquial conversation. Generally it is what can be referred to as public language. The major characteristic of this kind of speech, sometimes referred to as steno-language, is that it does not disclose any depth of meaning. It is closed. There is in its communication no openness to the realm of personal significance. It is, in Buber's term, I–It language.

Inner language, by contrast, has elements of disclosure in it. It is language that in a depth sense is involved with centres of human struggle such as relationship to other persons and to the physical world, and with such realities as love and hate, peace and war, life and death. It is open language, communal language, and in a curious way, private language. It is presentual language in the sense that its offering is one of presence. That presence, which invites a dialogue, introduces us to mystery and, properly, a sense of awe. It is I–Thou language. It is the language of mutuality, of communion.

Inner speech which invests the congregation's life with significance has several functions. The first is that it is communicating language, language that invites a loving struggle to know its fullest limits. It is interpreting language that confers meaning on significant events. It is the language of understanding that unveils the hidden layers of the structure of experience. It is feeling language, personal language, the language of crisis. It is committing language that requires a stance be taken toward the reality to which it makes testimony.

This language is both verbal-symbolic and non-verbal-symbolic. It is concerned with the power of words and the power of events, objects and gestures, for these 'speak' also.

It is possible for the language of inner speech to become merely denotive language from which the vitality has disappeared because it has lost touch with primary experience. It is also possible that what has existed in the congregation's life as outer language can be infused with a new spirit and burst into life. To give a congregation fresh and different words by which to tell their story is to introduce them to a new reality.

'SPEAKING' LANGUAGE

Language is the thread by which a system of associated commonplaces is bound together with meaning. Verbal-symbolic language therefore, when sought in its native undergrowth, is not to be discovered in the grammar of a universal language but in the rhythms of a particular language.

'Flatlanders cannot understand mountain people'. When an inhabitant of the Appalachian mountains in West Virginia makes a statement of this kind he is indicating through his words the presence of a threshold he sees as impenetrable. Language systems, as Tolkien believed, presuppose a mythic universe. The phrase 'Jesus saves' is one illustration of a complex myth of God's action in the world buried in two words brought into conjunction with each other. There are phrases which act as identifying symbols: 'just folks', 'the big smog', 'banana bender'. The religious persuasion of a group is detectable in their language: 'the Lord's people', 'a Spirit-filled community', 'doers of the Word', 'Bible-believing Christians'.

In one community 'salvation' is the dominant symbol of their faith, in another 'reconciliation', in a third 'unity in the love of peace', and in yet another, 'sharing'. Listening carefully to the language in pulpit and pew, in one congregation one will hear the language of pastoral care and group dynamics. In the next congregation, organisational development and systems language will hold the key. Here is a congregation at home with the language of Canaan interspersed with the cadences of the King James translation of the Bible. There the 1662 prayer book remains the language of faith.

In every congregation there is a circumscribing imagery, clusters of words that limit and de-limit. A visit to a farming community will furnish illustrations of rural metaphors. The wisdom of my father's generation was full of them. 'Distant fields are greener.' 'No use locking the barn door after the horse has bolted.' 'You can lead a horse to water but you can't make him drink.' By contrast the imagery of an inner-city congregation concerned for urban renewal and social justice can be filled with words like 'praxis', 'bourgeois morality', 'oppressive majority', 'suffering servant'.

The language of youth groups reflects the electronic and silicon-chip revolutions. 'Switched on', 'turned off', 'spaced out' – the list is endless. For many of the young, silence and reverence are alien modes of experience. The slow movement of the liturgy does not mesh with the flow of their consciousness, and the words used, which presuppose participation in its inner reality, are neither communicating, interpreting or committing for them. It does not hold their story.

In one congregation, by a study of the language, students were able to identify the past orientation of the congregation. 'The symbolic word used when talking about the church appears to be "then", or some other word that refers to the past.' It was inevitable that many of the young people in the congregation had long since ceased to attend a community that offered them nothing but nostalgia for the past.

These illustrations of various language fashions or preferences are not of themselves informing. What is revealing are the central symbolic words that define the people and fashion their identity. They are words that speak of the return of the separated to integration and wholeness. They are words that tell of vindication beyond the present conflicts of life. They are words that honour integrity and look for its transformation. They are words that focus on the nature of forgiveness and the transforming reality of love. These are the words of faith and hope that relate to that of which nothing more can or need be said.

These central symbols hold the story of the people. It is that story into which they project themselves and from which they gain strength and assurance. Sometimes the poverty of a congregation's verbal-symbolic language is crushing. At other times it seems fatally diseased, having lost all contact with its roots. There are places where the language crackles with intensity and throbs with vitality. And others where it is so much a part of being human that to identify it is to destroy it. Its efficacy lies in its hiddenness and gentility. To listen to the words the people use is to be educated in who they are.

NON-VERBAL LANGUAGE

'The Lord whose oracle is at Delphi neither speaks nor conceals but gives signs.' So Heraclitus wrote. The Lord of whom the Bible speaks also communicates by signs. But the proper sense is not merely of a sign but of a symbol which evokes something of the richness, wonder and mystery of the Christian story. 'A symbol owes its symbolic character to the fact that it stands for something other than, or at least more than, what it immediately is.'[5]

'The symbol reveals certain aspects of reality . . . which defy any other means

71

of knowledge. Images, symbols and myths are not irresponsible creations of the psyche; they . . . fulfil a function, that of bringing to light the most hidden modalities of being.[6] The symbols that carry meaning for a particular people can be various. They can include a sequence of events, a person, ritual gestures, any object that reveals the numinous, present in their experience.

The breaking of bread and the drinking of wine remains a central act in the Christian Church.[7] In particular congregations the eucharist can be the pre-eminent symbol of God's present act or of little significance relative to other activities. Where communion is not celebrated frequently it is unlikely that the meaning associated with the act is determinative in the people's self-understanding. But not necessarily so. It can be out of reverence, not neglect, that holy communion is celebrated only once a month. The local practice has its own rationale.

The complexity of the language system of a congregation can cloak as well as illumine what is essentially there. On more than one occasion students have discovered that what gains attention is not necessarily of central significance for a people. Sometimes the symbol's power is located at an unexpected level. A case in point was a communion table which had been used in a Methodist Church. When a decision was made by the founders of the congregation to build a church a plot of land was purchased which had on the site a number of trees. One of the members of the congregation took the wood from these trees and made the communion table, which in itself was a symbol of the people's hope, as much as what happened on its surface when communion was held. The two ideas were inextricably intertwined.

The deep-seated power of this symbol however remained largely at the level of unspoken acceptance. When the Uniting Church came into being, it was decided to sell the Methodist Church building. The people moved to join a former Presbyterian community to make a united congregation. The communion table accompanied them but, because it was not needed, was stored in the church hall. Some time after the union the repertory group of the congregation, looking for a table as a prop in their new play, hauled out the communion table and used it. The action caused deep hurt in those who remembered what it meant in the pilgrimage of the former Methodist group.

The story illustrates not only how an object can be the warrant of a people's faith but how a symbol can be hidden in the life of the people and seldom addressed directly as such. It also illustrates how others can be oblivious to the meaning dimension which is part of their shared life. Just as a photograph album can reveal what is never spoken, so can the living symbols of a congregation tell their story more forcibly than words alone. In the case of two congregations coming together, part of the process of creating a common history is the sharing of the photograph albums of the past. Marriages always require a creative negotiation of past history and loyalties in order that present and future can achieve their genuine possibilities. The coincidence of verbal and non-verbal symbolic language is one of those educational issues that needs to be given serious attention by clergy. The opposition of spoken word and symbolic gesture can fragment the meaning system of the congregation so severely that it becomes a culture of silence, unable to share what it most deeply believes.

THE PROBLEM OF SUPERIMPOSED LANGUAGE

History has many illustrations of the power that is released when people can share the faith in their own spoken tongue: Wyclif and the translation of the Bible into yeoman English; Meister Eckhart who spoke in the folk-culture of the German people thus bringing faith out of the prison of scholarly Latin; Martin Luther and the opening of the notion of priesthood for all believers, itself a symbolic act of considerable power uniting word and action in a new understanding of our relationship to God. Compare C.S. Lewis: 'We must learn the language of our audience. And let me say at the outset that it is no use at all in saying a priori what the "plain man" does or does not understand. You have to find out by experience . . . You must translate every bit of your theology into the vernacular.'[8]

Listening to the preaching of many clergy leads to the conclusion that the language of the pulpit is one which is superimposed on the people's experience. Its source lies outside their present world however revered it may be in tradition. Often it is the vocabulary of the seminary, and of particular theologians honoured in that seminary. There is a hunger in the people to understand what it means, but very often its complexity escapes them because it does not enter the communication system of their local habitats and sojournings. To hear the people means also to listen to the language they use to communicate with each other. It means acquiring a new vocabulary in order to speak to the centres of meaning that tell them who they are. It means affirming the pregnant imagery, not only of the Bible but of their own conversation.

The art of spoken language is to address the people out of the intimacy of the historic faith, where they themselves know the present intimacy of God. When that happens it can be said of us also, 'your words have kept people on their feet'.

INTIMACY

The dimension of intimacy in the life of a congregation is intertwined with the dimensions of time, space and language already discussed. In the case of time, the longer one participates in the life of a community the deeper the identification and the greater the sense of intimacy. With the category of space, intimacy is related to 'dwelling in' and associating significance with being 'there' together with others. Those who have attended class reunions from thirty years ago will recognise how intimacy is lacking although memories and location may be shared in common. The nature of intimacy relates to 'being with' and 'dwelling in' of a consistent kind. It is constantly renewed by sharing in events, and learning to trust what your particular community is for you.

The language of faith is also important in the idea of intimacy because it offers metaphors and images that are inclusive and welcoming. The imagery employed by the church is personal and communal. God is talked of as Father, Mother, Shepherd, Provider. Jesus is guide, pioneer, friend and master. The church is mother, home, sanctuary and family. There are other images that are not images immediately informed by intimacy, but they offer by contrast an alternative horizon to the idea of intimacy.

Intimacy is always in polar tension with the idea of distance. The mystery of mutual distance is as important as the mystery of intimacy. Distance is not necessarily cold, while intimacy is warm. Rather it is the necessary counter-point to intimacy which gives intimacy its strength and corrects its excesses. To talk of intimacy is to include distance and to honour it as part of the rhythm of separated uniqueness in tension with community. The paradox is that the further one travels with others the more personal and the more unique each life becomes. There lies here a fundamental mystery which serves only to illustrate the importance of the idea of intimacy in the essential being of any community.

INTIMACY AND ETHOS

What is included in the idea of intimacy is what is generally referred to as the ethos of the congregation. The ethos of a congregation is 'the tone, character, and quality of their life, its moral and aesthetic style and mood – and their world view – the picture they have of the way things in sheer actuality are, their most comprehensive ideas of order'.[9]

The ethos reflects the way the people's experience is structured and has its most powerful expression in the sentiment associated with belonging. Currents of feeling, shifts of mood, a buoyancy of spirit are the centre of what forms the ethos of a congregation. At the heart of it all is the dimension of intimacy which infuses the feeling tone of the public celebrations of the congregation. It is the ethos of a congregation that is guardian of its inner life. Where that inner life is centred and bonded, the ethos of the community is a palpable force capable of great good and able to resist assaults of all kinds on the morale and spirit of the people. Because the ethos of the community is multi-dimensional its very strength can be understood by a close examination of the dimension of intimacy. It is intimacy at the pre-conscious and unconscious levels of community experience which brings coherence and unity out of much that otherwise would remain incoherent and fragmentary.

THREE FACETS OF INTIMACY

The word, intimacy, comes from a Latin root meaning to declare, or put in. Common usage also provides us with a notion of closeness, which, if it defies precise articulation, at least points to a state of relationship that bears the weight of communion at a deeper level.

Three ways of pursuing the dimension of intimacy in the life of a congregation suggest themselves.

The first is the idea of intimacy as closeness, the indicators of which can be detected in the psychological climate operating in a community. Any person sensitive to psychological climate is quickly able to read the temperature that is stable and customary in a community's life.

The second is intimacy as depth. This sense of intimacy relates to the intrinsic nature of community life and the love which gives meaning to the whole.

The third idea of intimacy is intimacy as commitment. This sense relates to the volitional nature of faith with its characteristic of announcing and declaring what is binding upon a community in its fundamental tasks and responsibilities.

1. *Intimacy as closeness*

The temptation of this category of intimacy is to see only the psychological components of closeness with others. While the psychological climate is important, what is more fundamental is the notion of proximity or distance from the community's centres of meaning. It is the centres of meaning that define the community as a community. Without the reference of intimacy to these centres and their unique shaping force, the local congregation can seem to be no different from the local Rotary or Country club. 'Camaraderie' is not intimacy but its substitute.

Intimacy as closeness can be expressed in a variety of ways. It can be detected in what evokes laughter and occasions silence. It is present where caring takes place or in the way people are acknowledged. It is seen in the people's readiness to share what they have, who they identify with, and how they express their sense of belonging. The test of a congregation's intimacy relates to the manner in which it includes its children. On the birth of a baby a rose may appear on the altar, when a death occurs there may be a period of silence. Gifts are exchanged upon confirmation, hugs at a baptism, and congratulations at a wedding.

There is no one simple test of intimacy, no single mode of its appearing. But it is open, inclusive and accepting. An illustration of this characteristic was demonstrated for me at a congregational gathering which was riven with conflict. An elderly member of the congregation, one of its original members and now in the minority age group, stood to make testimony of what she believed. The language was the language of the revival meeting, the tone imperative. But the congregation listened her out in a respectful silence. Later when seeking the source of this acceptance I learned that the speaker was held in great esteem in the congregation because she had been the guardian of its history, a shepherd of its meaning into the present. 'We listen because we know she loves us.' To a stranger that sentiment came as a surprise. But for the people it was as accepted a consensus as existed among them.

It is also distressing to observe how a sense of belonging can be destroyed by the use of exclusive language. Many women feel disenfranchised by the language of the church. People who are divorced, separated or widowed feel rejection when the church assumes the nuclear family as the sanctioned model for child raising. The absence of forgiveness and the acceptance that is part of it comes as a blow to those who seek from the church a word of reassurance. In many congregations such blindness to the needs and circumstances of its members can prohibit the growth of intimacy, not the least because such practice runs counter to its professed faith.

2. *Intimacy as depth*

In focusing upon the centres of meaning which inform a congregation's life, attention is directed to that which is recognised as exercising an ultimate claim on the people. The centres of meaning in a congregation focus on what is loved and cherished above all else.

The moment of receiving bread and wine contains a fundamental pattern of giving and receiving, of need and response, of love expressed and hope renewed. To watch the faithful on this moving occasion is to touch depths of intimacy that can only be described by words such as faith, hope, love and mystery.

This quality of depth can be discerned at festival times such as harvest thanksgiving; at events that constitute a rite of passage such as confirmation or first communion; on occasions of great sadness such as death. When a people gather to celebrate the harvest in a rural community the activities of love and work are related to a cosmic frame which honours the seasons and dependence upon a bountiful God. A sense of unity and joy transfuses the festival. The essential meaning of the people's life is shared dramatically.

Similarly the death of a revered member of the community can reveal what is regarded as fundamental. In a letter a student wrote to tell how the Saturday bowls competition had been cancelled because of a death in the town. In small rural settings where there is no sustained distinction between church and the general life of the town, the whole community mourns as one family. What is revealed on such occasions is the presence of a profound intimacy which surges up into ritual response. The limit situation, represented by catastrophe, plague, natural disaster and death, is the mid-wife that brings to visible life the essential confession of the people.

It is on occasions of great joy and great sadness that people are freed to talk about what moves them most completely. They are moments when a congregation can find words to express what their common life means. Such occasions not only reveal the intimacy at the centre of the congregation's life, they testify to the ineffable mystery at the heart of the faith of the church.

3. Intimacy as commitment

One of the central ideas in the derivation of the word intimacy is that of announcing or declaring. When an engagement occurs the intimacy shared by the couple is publicly announced and a declaration of intention is made. The commitment implied is a natural expression of intimacy itself. There is in the relationship a knowledge of the other which only intimacy can give. It is at once a revealing and a binding of persons to each other.

The devotion of a congregation to its own story not only announces its commitment but also indicates the areas of responsibility it accepts. One congregation had combined both of these elements in a memorial garden that was placed between the church and its auxiliary buildings. To move from one to the other meant passing through the garden in which the ashes of past members were buried. The garden was a source of memory which spoke of the committed lives of those who had lived and died in the faith, as well as a reminder of the present commitment of the people to bear witness to that faith which had guided those now dead.

Founders day, saints day, all souls day, are moments in the rhythm of the liturgical year that give opportunity for declaring anew the commitment of the people. In the practice of Methodist congregations a covenant service is still held on New Year's Eve to confess an intention about the year ahead. The commitment so celebrated and confessed addresses the centres of meaning which define the identity of the people. When a congregation announces an intention to direct its life it is, at the same time, sharing an intimacy which makes the people one. To observe what the people confess together as their mission gives a clear path to what they regard as essential. The nature of that commitment varies from congregation to congregation.

In one congregation a student observed symbols referring to the world as one world. Through listening to the people, reading notice sheets and looking at the church budget he noticed a concern for countries of the Third World. He was able to understand what this pointed to at an annual service, which was a high festival occasion in the particular congregation, when pledges were made 'to give as much as we can to further our vision of one world under God'. The percentage of the church budget devoted to mission activity and aid programs was considerably higher than he had seen in any other church. The church had a well-established tradition of missionary service.

LANGUAGE AND INTIMACY

The idea of intimacy pursued here as closeness, depth and commitment is inevitably associated with the total experience of a people's shared life. It is intimacy that gives particular colouring or tone to the personal and social stories in which we find our lives enfolded. The ethos it gives rise to can have a dominant thrust or direction. It is not without its own ambiguity, for the shadow and light of intimacy is not experienced apart from our moods or concerns.

It is the product of past history, of events in time and space. This ethos is brokenly communicated in the language of a people. It is always elusive because it is not constant but flowing language, carrying imperfectly the quality and affect of shared life. It is possible for the intimacy of a congregation's life to sour into hostility and to spell rejection to those who are outside its life. Just as language can become exclusive, so intimacy can remain restricted and partisan.

That is why the warning of David Kelsey needs to be heeded. 'The activities comprising the common life of a Christian worshipping community should all be ordered to one end, viz., shaping the identities of its members so that their forms of speech and action will publicly enact in the world the mission to which the community is called and by which it is defined.'[10]

In seeking to understand the function of language and intimacy, their influence on the identity of the people has to be related directly to the centres of meaning which testify to God's renewing action. But without understanding these two dimensions little can be done in the process of guiding the congregation to a fuller possession and confession in word and deed of what it is, and is yet to be.

NOTES TO CHAPTER 5

1. Quoted from the *Selected Writings of Edward Sapir*, University of California Press,1949, p.162, by Max Black, *Models and Metaphors*, Cornell University Press, Ithaca, New York, 1962, p.245. Black includes an extensive discussion of the linguistic theories of Benjamin Lee Whorl and Edward Sapir which has been of considerable help in the development of the position of language in this chapter. See Black on the 'Sapir-Whorl Hypothesis' in *Models and Metaphors*.

2. Quoted by Max Black in *Models and Metaphors*, p.252.

3. Cousins, Ewart H. (ed.) *Process Theology*: 'Faith and the Formative Image of our Time' Meland, New York: Newman Press, 1971, p.38.

4. ibid., p.37-38.

5. Wheelwright, Phillip. *The Burning Fountain*, Bloomington and London: Indiana University Press, 1968, p.6. Used by permission.

6. Eliade, Mircea. *Images and Symbols*, trans. Philip Mairet, London: Harvill Press, 1961, p.57.

7. 'It is in the elemental action of eating that we make our fundamental decisions about what we mean by shalom'. Walter Brueggemann, *Living Toward a Vision*, United Church Press, Philadelphia, 1976, p.75. Brueggemann also notes that covenant making in the Old Testament is characteristically done by covenant meal (Exodus 24:11).

8. From *God in the Dock*, copyright© 1970 by C.S. Lewis Pte Ltd, reproduced by permission of Curtis Brown Ltd., London.

9. Geertz, Clifford, *The Interpretation of Cultures*, New York: Basic Books, 1973, p.89. © Tavistock Publications Ltd., London. Used by permission.

10. Kelsey, David H. 'The Bible and Christian Theology' in *Journal of the American Academy of Religion*, September 1980, p.37. See also pp.385-402.

CHAPTER SIX

Consensus and Circumstance

W*HAT POINTS OF CONSENSUS BIND THE PEOPLE? WHAT DO THEY admit or prohibit? What are the circumstances that shape the congregation? Which factors of circumstance are inevitable? Which capable of being changed?*

Every community shares structural elements that hold the community together. Time, space, language and intimacy are some of these elements which, in their inter-relatedness with each other, define the particular social reality of a community. The community acknowledges the influence of those dimensions of its life by a common recognition of what is agreed or accepted among them to be the truth about themselves and their world. It is this agreement which the word consensus embraces, and it relates most directly to the belief systems that define the character and direct the intentionality of the community. As intimacy is to ethos, so consensus is to belief system.

CONSENSUS

The word 'consensus' has currency in the fields of medicine, law and ecclesiology. In the medical world it is understood as that co-operation or sympathy that exists in various parts of an organism. In law, it is used to refer to unanimity in matters of opinion, evidence or testimony. In the case of the church it is held to refer to a formal statement of belief, or a confession. The Latin root holds two central ideas: agreement together and feeling together. That is why the word consensus is so useful when concern is directed to the meaning level of a congregation. It can search out the accord in a community that recognises both its external and internal dimensions.

At the level of meaning and faith, that which people feel together is the most determinative force in their shared existence. In the area of consensus, beliefs are those convictions which are shared, persistent, internally linked, acknowledged in corporate acts, and call forth commitment. This concord of sentiment and belief cannot be defined precisely nor is it the possession of a single person. The boundaries are imprecise. But general definitions are possible.

'A belief system is a set of related ideas (learned and shared) which has some permanence, and to which individuals and/or groups exhibit some commitment.'[1]

What gives substance to that which is believed is the ideology of the community, the attitude taken to its history and significant events, and the value attached to particular people and acts which have become normative for the people's identity.

There are four components that help define the authority of any belief system. The first is its capacity to confer and define value. The second is the criteria it provides that gives validity to the corporate acts and shared rituals of the people. A third function of a belief system is the perspective it offers by which events and experiences are processed and ordered. Finally it offers a language which enables communication and denotes what is significant and true.

In any community what is believed is largely taken for granted, for it is one and the same with the pattern of shared life. To the participant what is agreed upon has an inherent stability, coherence, and congruence because he/she has accepted that which is professed. It is seen as a true statement of the way things essentially are.

Consensus, however, is not the same thing as a belief system, for while a belief system may have a relative independence from daily events, the consensus of the people is constantly moving, changing and re-forming around the congregation's centres of meaning. Variation occurs within and between communities because of such factors as leadership patterns, openness to change and innovation, the relevance of accepted consensus to present events, the nature of the commitment demanded, the style of church life, the re-discovery of sources of generativity in the history of the community, and so on.

STRUCTURE AND BELIEF SYSTEM

Consensus, as it operates among a people, fulfils a number of functions. It defines boundaries, provides stability, grants status, confirms leadership and offers reassurance, to name some functions. But these functions are not of the same order. Granting status and offering reassurance are different kinds of functions although they are not unrelated. The difference arises from the fact that belief systems exist in two social contexts, related but separate. The first is the context of meaning which relates to the inner life of a congregation. The second context is that of social organisation which deals with the structure of the outer life of the congregation.

It is possible to see the tension between these dimensions of consensus by reference to the language appropriate to each context. The outer dimension is addressed by the language of organisation development. Words such as role, status, power, outcomes, authority, planned objectives, and critical path evaluation can be used to describe the outer consensual life of a people.

The inner dimension requires a different vocabulary. The words appropriate to the context of meaning are words like faith, values, communication, beliefs, commitments, confession, prayer – in short, the language elsewhere referred to as personal communal language. The tension between these language frames symbolises a tension at the heart of consensus itself. It is the opposition that arises between the useful skills necessary for administrative efficiency and the maintenance of the group on the one hand, and the vital inner expression of the people's life with its dreams, visions and unexpressed hopes on the other. A sympathetic compatibility between the outer and inner dimensions of consensus is necessary for the health of the congregation.

If a choice has to be made, however, it is the contention of the position held in this book that the inner dimension is prior and determinative because it is concerned with the realm of meaning and the domain of faith. 'At the table as nowhere else we are made aware that true life is in mystery and not in management.'[2] From a purely prudential point of view, to use power to force change will fail, in the long term, if the attitudes and sentiment associated with unspoken consensual matters are not addressed.

Organisation change will always be judged either worthy or not by the deeply held sentiment of the people. Much bruising conflict can be avoided in the recognition that consensus has within its gift two dimensions which can be set, like Cain and Abel, into fatal opposition with each other. The symbiotic relationship between the two contexts, that of meaning and organisation, has significant consequences. As Freud observed, in a given social system as the number of normatively defined interactions increases, the number of spontaneously defined interactions decreases.' Further, as Turner observes,

'Structure is all that holds people apart, defines their differences, and constrains their actions, including social structure in the British anthropological sense.'[3] If the alienating consequences of an abstract system, defined by structural relationships, is to be overcome, then the congregation must be viewed as a living whole, always defined by its symbols of faith and the meaning that is derived from them. The integrating principle is not order but intuition. If faith is primary, its nature must be honoured in the way we nurse the agreed consensus it gives birth to in the congregation.

CONSENSUS AND CONFLICT

Consensus has its normal effect by a persisting moral influence which determines what is permitted or accepted. The norms, as inflexible as steel girders, that include as well as exclude, are not always consciously regarded but operate beneath the surface of communal interaction. When conflict breaks out in a congregation the 'agreed-upon' norms are threatened and brought dramatically into view.

'Conflicts seem to bring fundamental aspects of society, normally overlaid by the customs and habits of daily intercourse, into frightening prominence. People have to take sides in terms of deeply entrenched moral imperatives and constraints, often against their own personal preferences. Choice is overborne by duty.'[4]

Conflict usually confirms accepted norms in the minds of those frightened by conflict, and therefore can operate as a source of exasperation to those who wish earnestly for change. Conflict unveils much of what is taken for granted. It can be the means of revealing what in other circumstances would remain hidden. The value of conflict from this perspective is its ability to open up possibilities for change, and to reveal where educative ventures should be directed. Openings for ministry are not less opportunities because they are discovered in a climate of hostility. The possibilities that are unearthed by conflict can lead to a recognition that conflict, properly processed, can be an indispensable aid in identifying what is regarded as fundamental and unchanging by a congregation.

The warrants for personal and communal participation are sanctioned by consensus. Much that is now consensual had a painful birth. A great deal depends therefore on the understanding and perspective of those who stand as mid-wives in situations of conflict.

THREE ASPECTS OF CONSENSUS

It has proved useful to seek out the operative presence of consensus by reference to three aspects of the life of a congregation. These are (1) nurture, (2) mission and (3) authority.

1. *Consensus as nurture*

Put simply, consensus as nurture refers to how we care for ourselves as a community. Norms exist that control the way people are included, and differences are handled. Decisions are made about how critical information will be distributed, and on the networks of communication which test out or confirm the consensus.

In one parish where I was the minister a decision was made by the elders meeting, all male, to undertake a stewardship campaign after no small amount of pressure from the chair. It was agreed that the meeting should reconvene two weeks later to work out details of the decision. I was the only person who turned up at that meeting. Inquiries revealed that when the men returned from their meeting on the first occasion and told their wives of the decision a reaction set in. The telephone wires ran hot and the wives reversed the decision. The network of communication in the congregation was controlled by the wives, as were most decisions in the home about money. Although the decision to proceed was finally confirmed, it had first to be negotiated through the informal networks of decision-making that existed in the congregation. A salutary lesson indeed.

What is *valued* is implicit in the decision-making mechanisms of the congregation. The care and support of children in a congregation reveals this, either positively or negatively, by reaction to the Sunday school and ministry with children. There is often a lack of consensus on this matter between clergy and the people.

Similarly, what is *believed* and why is part of the notion of consensus and nurture. It is not in terms of individual religious conviction only but also in relation to the life of the congregation that agreement is reached.

To illustrate, one congregation studied seemed to have given tacit acceptance to a number of propositions about its life. These propositions were generally voiced by older members and on important occasions by the former Session Clerk who spoke with an authority conferred on him by the others. Four strong currents of opinion, held to be true, were identified by students. The first was that religious faith was a private matter. The second, the parish was a dying parish. Thirdly, the people recognised no claim on their loyalty or energies but that of their own fraternity. They were determinedly parochial, and defensive. The fourth opinion was that faith was intellectual understanding. The expression of feelings of any kind in a public manner was taboo. The total effect was to close out all new possibilities. The consensus operated as a self-fulfilling prophecy.

Consensus can relate to how people dress, the correct way of worshipping, even to the furnishing of the church buildings. In some places norms exist which prohibit public recognition of conflict for the sake of peace. In others all matters related to the political-economic axis of life, matters of social equity and justice, are proscribed. How we order our own house tells a great deal about who we are.

2. *Consensus as mission*

A community such as the local church, which acknowledges a responsibility for others, has to deal with the ways in which that responsibility should be carried out. At bottom, this question is a question of the relationship between faith and culture. It involves making decisions about the movement from within the congregation to missionary activity outside it.

It is not uncommon in this regard to encounter a firm consensus that the issue of mission is best undertaken by individual Christians who, dispersed into the community, operate there as leaven to transform the whole. One church dealt with a Billy Graham campaign by placing more stewards at the door to welcome the converts who were likely to come to church.

Behind such thinking lies a view that within the church there is light and beyond is darkness. Essentially no mission as a community is seriously contemplated because the consensus is world-denying and mission is left to individuals who act alone in the public arena.

Consensus about the nature of the community determines the outcomes of the congregation's planning for mission. Implicitly a stance is taken to the relationship with the surrounding neighbourhood. There is always an unspoken agreement about the relationship between those inside the community and those outside. The typology offered by Richard Niebuhr is a significant resource in determining what the congregation will permit in its missionary activity and the assumptions held about the relationship of those outside the fellowship to those inside.[5]

The services offered by a congregation in themselves bear testimony to the self-understanding a congregation has. They reflect values, their objectives define relationships, the roles undertaken relate to the expression of authority. The structures created to effect welfare efforts tell a story about what the congregation is agreed upon and how it views itself.

The possibilities and limitations of different societies are important in this context. In Africa the church is a centre for education, health and physical shelter. A separation between the private and public domain does not exist in any recognisable equivalent to the pattern in most Western countries. To preach the gospel is to be concerned with the total fabric of human life in society.

By contrast, it is possible to discover in a congregation in the West a consensus about the missionary outreach of the church which is focused in raising money to support missionaries overseas. It is at the point of a community's relationship with others that consensus about identity and task can be discerned. For many congregations their struggle to relate the political-economic axis to the socio-religious axis constitutes the most painful continuing uncertainty of their shared existence.

3. *Consensus as authority*

The two areas of nurture and mission, and the consensus that exists about care of the self and the neighbour, is mediated by the consensus that exists about authority. Authority in a community is invested in a number of critical centres. These include sanctioned roles, symbolic functions, particular persons and traditional practices.

Most of these are supported by reference to scripture or historical orthodoxy. The issue of power, which is central in any community, always has to be mediated between competing interest groups. The structures developed in a local congregation are there not only to establish order but to resolve conflict and uncertainty. In the interaction between persons and groups a community throws up workable resolutions to deal with the conflict of differing points of view. The resolutions are confirmed by agreement, and while open from time to time to negotiation, they are normally regarded as binding on all equally.

A newcomer is likely to be greeted in the first weeks with a response like, 'we always do it that way'. Doing it that way has become self-evident. Often the practice represents a resolution of a power struggle such as an agreement that the children of the Sunday school will never come into the worship service if the minister never comes into the Sunday school. This agreement had been reached in one congregation to resolve a long standing struggle between a Sunday school superintendent and a minister.

Similar areas of consensus can be identified like the common trade-off in which the minister can make all the decisions in return for which the congregation remain passive, with no real intention of carrying the decisions out.

In the area of authority all that is spontaneous, immediate, concrete and unstructured comes into conflict with that which is ordered, abstract, predictable and normative. When a conflict erupts over whether the youth group can run a dance on Saturday night in the parish hall or play tennis on the church courts on Sunday, it is likely that matters of consensus are at issue.

Whatever decision is made, it is inevitable that it will be tested by the community, not in terms of its external consequences only, but whether the very essence of the community is under threat. The real task is to overcome the separation of thought and feeling which involves also the tension between structure and value. The task is both theological and educational.

CIRCUMSTANCE

Circumstance like the other categories of time, space, language, intimacy and consensus, is capable of operating at a number of levels. Circumstance can include social factors, geographical features, physical characteristics, ethnic composition and economic status. Its major function in these terms is to describe what can be called environmental factors.

Circumstance however, according to Webster's dictionary, is 'the sum of essential and environmental factors'. In this understanding, circumstance has reference not just to accidental but to essential dimensions of a people's life. This definition includes the idea of a state of being, an essential condition such as is suggested by Shakespeare's line, 'Time, matter and other circumstance.' It suggests an interaction between daily events and a deeper ground of meaning. Circumstance, when it 'stands around' is, in this broader sense, far more than 'happenstance'.

ENVIRONMENTAL FACTORS

Every community is shaped to a significant degree by the events in its life which always relate to particular places or locations. As Siegfried Giedon put it, 'the slow shaping of daily life is of equal importance to the explosions of history'.

Congregations can dwindle in size and grow in age. Inner rings of the city can be abandoned for a cherished outer suburbia, only to be wooed again as housing and prices for essential services force young people to regenerate those areas once ignored.

Ethnic patterns can change in the neighbourhood. Real estate values soar or plummet dramatically. Congregations can die under one leadership style and be reborn by another. Some communities become exclusive despite themselves while other communities struggle to achieve status. Falling numbers may force congregations to join together with a serious threat to identity as a consequence. A congregation can splinter and disagreement can harden into hostility.

A factory may close and make a congregation no longer economically viable. Harvests can fail that mean the death not only of a church but also a town. Every congregation is subject to the flux of change, the blind actions of chance, the tragedy of war, the heartless judgment of fate, the sadness of forced migration. These elements of circumstance are written into the story of every congregation. They shape the present reality and future expectations that a community has in its struggle to seize the possibilities of its life. However, communities differ in the way in which the circumstances of their life are addressed. It is in the nature of the different responses to environmental factors that the inner dimension of circumstance is discovered.

CIRCUMSTANCE AS INNER RESPONSE

There are many possible ways in which the response of a community to its circumstances can be explored. One possible pattern is to examine the life of the people along a spectrum from deprivation to affluence. Being poor is a significantly different state to being rich.

In the case of a local community the economic circumstances which shape its life can determine the nature of the people's response to the world. Three points along the spectrum of want and plenty can act as a guide. These are circumstance as (1) deprivation, as (2) balanced uncertainty and (3) abundance. From ministry to congregations along this spectrum, experience teaches that in each of these categories a congregation tells a story which seeks to give a rationale for the particular conditions of its life. The biblical traditions provide a fund of images that sustain hope and provide interpretations for the present experience of the people.

It is in the attempt to discern meaning in the prevailing situation that particular elements of the biblical story are selected. They are selected to meet the need of the people to identify God's action in the prevailing conditions of their present experience.

1. *Circumstance as deprivation*

Many congregations live out their life against a background of struggle and deprivation. The people, like the Israelites in the desert, travel with a promise not yet possessed rather than a promise fulfilled. They do not inhabit a land of milk and honey. Their hope is directed to that which is to come. They do not have what they need but their conviction is that the time is coming when God will act to bring his people into their inheritance. Hunger and lack will be no more. There was something of this expectation of God's *kairos* breaking forth in the present, with its promise of vindication of the people's suffering and travail, in the campaigns of Martin Luther King.

Congregations across the land welcomed that new state in which discrimination and economic deprivation would be lifted. Where coercion existed there would freedom make its appearance. Where hostility festered there would come peace. Where injustice bred despair there would be justice and hope.

It is not necessary to restrict the sense of deprivation to that of cruel political circumstances. Congregations in drought infested lands hope yearly for deliverance under God's hand. In some congregations there is a poverty of spirit that cripples the people. No leadership exists to call the people out of darkness into light. In another, memory of past glories can continue to flicker, the very nostalgia for what is gone bearing the hope that a flame will burst forth to herald a new day.

The image of death and resurrection is evoked in many congregations suffering under severe deprivation. So also the confession of the new creation born out of the old order and realised in God's act in Christ. These images and others like them, which make up the language of the people, reflect the struggle of their spirit to overcome the darkness of the present hour, a darkness which is but the shadow of circumstance cast on their way. In such conditions there is a cluster of images that afford a lustre and a brilliance that overcome the gloom of the present. There are stories that fit the need of the people that can and must be told. To serve a congregation in a state of deprivation requires not only a keen sense of the realities that press upon them, but also a sensitive reverence for the centres of meaning which are the bearers of new life, sometimes in the very presence of death itself.

2. Circumstance as balanced uncertainty

Most church congregations are composed of people who belong to that sector of society that Saul Alinsky referred to as 'the have a little and want mores'. Such congregations as a whole do not suffer tangible restrictions on their life from either the political or economic spheres. They are not in a survival situation. However, there is a fear of losing what has been gained by sober and diligent effort, and a desire to get more of those resources that eliminate the nagging uncertainty that the present situation is not permanent. What is an individual fear becomes communally expressed. Participation in the local congregation provides a warrant and justification for the style of life lived by its members.

There is an element of choice possible to most middle class congregations that is not available to 'have not' communities. On the one side there is a recognition of the privileges enjoyed. On the other there is a desire to have more of what seems a bare surplus above present needs.

The threat to congregations living in this between state is one of fragmentation. What is most prized is unity, even peace of mind, that deals satisfactorily with the tension of being in the middle. It is not to be wondered at that middle class congregations put such a premium on unity and fellowship. There is little foundation for security in an existence they fear is precarious. In the biblical story therefore individuals see their personal struggle dramatised and victoriously concluded. Not uncommonly that biblical perspective is selective and reduced to the comfortable words of Jesus.

Stated positively, the circumstances of such a community are drawn together by a vision that both confers upon the people their identity as God's people and reassures them in that identity. The story told that complements the circumstances of the congregation's life is a story of a covenant people who are loved despite their failures and trusted with responsibilities that test their strength. It is a story which deals with the tension of not minding too much and of minding enough. In each community the particular form and shape of the people's story reflects the enfolding grasp of circumstance. It is in searching out its hidden influence that an identity for the people can be forged.

3. Circumstance as abundance

A third focus of the category of circumstance is that of abundance. People who belong to affluent congregations know that they live in highly favourable circumstances. Their wealth and prestige enables the congregation to gain leadership of a high calibre. The congregation's needs can be met and its life sustained by programs and activities that address current concerns within the congregation. Welfare projects are prevalent. A newcomer can sense a satisfaction about the way things are. Commitments are met without strain; membership numbers, whether falling or rising, pose no immediate problem. People are agreed that they belong to a goodly fellowship.

In such cases, the style of liturgical life has more a celebration of the given about it than an expectation or anticipation of what God will yet do among them. The community already enjoys what other congregations aspire to and hope to achieve. In these circumstances the prevailing mythos is likely to focus on the integrity of the community's life with exhortation that it might be transformed into a more complete version of itself. The theology favoured is that which speaks of success, not of failure, for success is viewed as the guarantee of faithfulness.

Yet it can be just as troubling to be in the most favourable of circumstances as it is to be in the least favourable: the desire to keep things as they are can become crippling. Reference to the biblical story reminds the congregation of its responsibility for the widow, the orphan and the stranger within the gates. God always calls his people to address new tasks. Those who live in circumstances of abundance are disturbed by the biblical word which reminds them, 'we are expected to become what we are not'.

The acceptance of God's beneficence is always threatened by a doubt as to a judgment it may imply. The peace of God sought in separation from violent or hostile environments may be revealed to be not the shalom of God but a fraud. The oppression of congregations in a situation of abundance, while of a different kind to those in deprivation, can be no less fatal to the life of the spirit. The words of Jesus about what we can hear and not hear have their most forceful application for congregations in a situation of abundance.

WORKING WITH CIRCUMSTANCES

Each category of circumstance has its limitations and possibilities. The way in which circumstances are engaged is a reflection of the depth of the people's conviction about the providence and care of God. There are false interpretations of what circumstance means. When a seminary president tells a group of students, 'It is your responsibility to see the congregation functions in concert with the requirements of the General Assembly', the sense of what significantly shapes the life of a congregation is the particular tradition to which the congregation belongs. It does not have its starting point in the concrete, historical realities of the present hour but in a tradition which has become normative and seeks to be definitive in contemporary events.

This is not what is intended by circumstance as a dimension of a faith community. Circumstance is that category of experience which currently determines the people's shared life.

To work creatively with the situation, as it is perceived, is to find those biblical images that speak to the present reality of the congregation. The biblical images can be of judgment as well as hope, and often both together. The resources of faith can overcome the temptation to despair, and arrest the slide into meaninglessness. The word that brings restoration and hope is offered because of the very circumstances that control our situation. Faith comes to expression, sometimes through and sometimes in spite of the circumstances that shape us. In an age of high mobility and rising anxiety the clearest path to trust in God's action is to the celebration of that faith which overcomes the world in the midst of the circumstances of that world.

SUMMARY

The six categories of analysis – time, space, language, intimacy, consensus and circumstance – are seen as ways in which the underlying structure of a congregation can be understood. Just as a magnet drawn over iron filings reveals the lines of force present, so these categories can be used to indicate the essential relationship between the outer and inner experience of the life of a congregation. The questions, 'how do I understand the culture of a congregation?' and 'how is meaning experienced, appropriated, and expressed by the congregation?' can be answered to some degree by seeking out the hidden structure of a community against the six dimensions employed.

Experience in using the categories has shown that not all categories are equally helpful in trying to discern the direction and purpose of a congregation. One pastor wrote to say that in his first congregation, a rural parish, time and language had been most useful, and in his next congregation, space and consensus. Employing the categories is an exercise in creativity. The need to check perceptions is never done away with entirely, and therefore a principle of dialogue is assumed in the process of naming.

The first phase of naming a congregation's life is not adequate in itself to understand how the meaning patterns of a congregation might be interpreted by the people. Again, experience has revealed that the six categories so interpenetrate each other that to see them as distinct falsifies the wholeness of the culture. One leads into the next until a picture comes into focus. It is the one picture. But one dimension adds light, another depth of field, yet another colour, and a fourth the parameters that shape the total configuration. In composing the picture, timing and perception are equally important. Interpreting what is seen is the next important step.

It is worth repeating that an empirical starting point carries with it an assumption about how the action of God is to be discerned. Following Gabriel Moran, the starting point of revelation is the personal, relational, social and practical experience of people today.[6] The conclusion of Thomas Groome is also important. 'The purpose of naming our present and knowing our story is that we may have some freedom to imagine and choose our future.'[7]

NOTES TO CHAPTER 6

1. Borhek, James T. and Curtis, Richard F. *A Sociology of Belief*, New York, London, Sydney, Toronto: John Wiley and Sons, 1975, p.5. Used by permission.

2. Brueggemann, op. cit. p.143.

3. Turner, Victor. *Dramas, Fields and Metaphors*, Ithaca and London; Cornell University Press, 1974, p.43. Used by permission.

4. ibid., p.35.

5. Niebuhr, H. Richard *Christ and Culture*. 1st ed., New York: Harper, 1951. See also Rudge, Peter F. *Ministry and Management*, London: Tavistock, 1968, pp.32-33. Rudge offers a useful typology of the patterns of church life. His categories include traditional, charismatic, classical, human relations, and systemic, and are a companion set internally helpful for analysing the style of a congregation.

6. Moran, Gabriel. *The Present Revelation: the search for religious foundations*, New York: Herder and Herder, 1972, p.222.

7. Groome, op. cit. p.186.

PART THREE
INTERPRETING

CHAPTER SEVEN
Valuing the Past

*B*EFORE PROCEEDING IT MAY BE HELPFUL TO RECALL THE philosophical orientation about educating a people of God, already outlined in the preface.

The central thesis which directs the movement from naming to interpreting and on to remaking is that to educate a people of God is to call forth a community which by faith seeks to conform its life to the pattern of Christ and to embody in the style of that life a distinctively Christian confession about human existence.

The next phase, that of interpreting the data which has come from a sympathetic participation in the life of the congregation, is an inevitable extension of that mode of understanding which characterised the first phase, that of naming. Interpretation as it is used here is a process 'of bringing forth significance, of conveying meaning, of restoring symbols to life and eventually of letting new symbols emerge. Hermeneutics is the method of overcoming the distance between a knowing subject and an object to be known.'[1]

The emphasis in this definition on active engagement is important. It presupposes an exchange between a particular culture and those who seek to understand it in which a transforming process occurs. That exchange does not confer meaning upon, but rather calls meaning forth by creative interaction with the stories, myths and rituals of the people. The present frame of reference which guides the congregation's self-understanding is sharpened and enlarged by a recovery of those past resources that have shaped the community's life.

In order to make such a perspective more than theoretical several focusing concepts are here offered. For no matter how much we agree with statements like 'a person will be immersed in the Christian story, the patterns of living, the rituals and symbols, and the actions and mission of the faith community, to experience how faith is defined and how life is given meaning',[2] we are no closer to knowing *how* we might understand that process in concrete, operational terms. Nor are we any closer to indicating how an intervention can be made into this stream of awareness in order to redirect its course.

The intention behind the employment of focusing concepts is to deal with some of the criticism already acknowledged. 'While representatives state that the faith community approach is a dialectic of transmission and transformation, it is difficult for them to state how this process of transformation occurs.'[3]

The structure of the next three chapters is dependent on the time experience of a congregation's life. The task is first to enable a community, with conscious intent, to value the past it has lived. The second facet of the enterprise is to assist in a claiming of the present. The final movement is that of helping the people seek a future that they affirm together.

The present chapter is concerned with the effort to lead a congregation into a positive valuing of their own past history. Several ways of doing that are now to be described. The first is to uncover the difference between remembered history and actual history and ask the question: Why is it so? The second is to recover the hero stories that live in the conscious memory of the people. The third is to dig out those artifacts of significance that carry a mysterious power to evoke wonder and awe in the present moment.

REMEMBERED HISTORY

To examine the history of a congregation by reference to its written documents is to learn that there is a significant gap between actual history and remembered history. That in itself is not surprising. People's memories are notoriously inaccurate. If you ask someone whether last winter was severe or not they are likely to reply, not by comparing last winter with previous winters, but in terms of their personal experience of last winter. If they had a bout of influenza, or were prevented from doing normal things by heavy rain, judgment about the weather will be made from the perspective of remembered discomforts.

So also a congregation. In every congregation there are originating occasions, generative events, that are remembered because they carry special significance for the people. What is recalled as important is 'that special occasion which provides us with an image by means of which all the occasions of personal and common life become intelligible'.[4] These special occasions are those events in the inner life of the congregation which shed light on the rest of the shared history and so give it meaning and purpose. They are revelatory moments that release energy in the life of the people.

By inviting people to share their memories of significant events and comparing the memories with the actual history of the community, what continues as living memory can be identified and the generative centres of meaning isolated. The questions follow. What is the power present in these events? What do they symbolise? How do they continue to work in the life of the people? What meaning do they carry for the congregation?

It is intriguing, for example, to enter a parish and discover that of the six clergy who had ministered to the community only two are ever spoken about in general conversation. A student in a situation of this kind asked of the different people he met why they told stories mostly of a minister of twenty years ago. Was it because they were avoiding present circumstances?

Associated with the incumbency of the particular minister was a redefinition of the ministry of the congregation so that it became in its own eyes a missioning congregation to the surrounding community. The warrant for the past twenty years service of the parish lay in the originating events of the early years of that ministry. Those who followed only served to sustain the myth of 'a serving community', not to recast it.

The identification of significant events can also lead to the identification of the periods of silence. In such periods it is possible on occasions to discover an unspoken agreement to suppress what happened at that time. One period of silence in a congregation was caused by the failure of the people to deal with the divorce of the minister and his leaving the church with a member of the choir. That period in the life of the church had become frozen. No processes undertaken had dealt creatively with the pain and hurt. A sensitive re-negotiation of the events of that time was the means of freeing the congregation of guilt and anger, and enabled the people to accept openly a period of their history that had not reached, until that moment, a satisfactory closure.

To work constructively with the memory of the congregation involves learning of the joys and sorrows, the loves and hates, the hopes and fears. These can be recovered by examining the gap between what is honoured and cherished as the continuing story, and what is forgotten and discarded for want of revelatory significance. It is an irony that sometimes the recovery of what was once regarded as unimportant fills the people with a renewed understanding. Past events have the capacity to gain immense contemporary value when what they represent is reappropriated and appreciated from the perspective of the present.

The examination of remembered history against recorded history is one of great value, for it can remind the people of what they have forgotten, and re-affirm them in who they are. It is a means of focusing the people's story, and interpreting that narrative in the context of Christian faith.

HERO STORIES

'Every culture or tradition lives by the compelling stories of its heroes. . . They illuminate new ways of being Christian, new ways of accepting and understanding Christian life. Their lives awaken new insight into the values of their tradition.'[5] We tell the stories of our heroes and heroines because in so doing we are able to appropriate the central hope of our present pilgrimage. They act as exemplars for us, paradigms of faith, in which by memory and repetition, we shape our lives by their example.[6]

In the Christian story there are people like Abraham, Moses, David, and pre-eminently Jesus who is the ritual folk hero, the archetype of faith. But the story does not end there. History has thrown up others who model for us the life of faith. From the disciples and St. Paul to the present, hero stories are told and retold. Different traditions honour different saints and heroes. The Lutherans honour Martin Luther; the Presbyterians, Calvin and Knox; the Methodists, John Wesley; Black Americans, Martin Luther King.

A listener in a local congregation will hear some of these names, and not others. There will also be names in the catalogue of saints that are, for the most part, anonymous outside the congregation. There are saints in every congregation whose lives have been or are a paradigm of what living faithfully means.

They are more than culture-bearing elites in Weber's phrase because, while their outer journey may gather the aspirations of a people, it is the point at which their lives touch the inner collective life of the people that their true power is set free. It is the inner journey that relates to the mystery of being.

When people are tempted to turn aside it is the image of the person loved and revered who calls them back: a faithful Sunday school teacher, the door steward who was there to greet people every Sunday for thirty years, the lay leader of the congregation who led the people on a march to the city hall to protest repressive legislation, the quiet spirituality of a now blind retired missionary, the founding father who bought an old abandoned church, had it moved and began a new congregation. There are countless stories of men and women whose lives have kindled in others the spark of faith.

One such story was of a minister long remembered after his death. They told of how this minister would chop wood for pensioners' fires, and arrange for meals when people were sick. He was immediately on the spot when a death occurred. He could be relied on to think of something when a difficulty arose. It was summed up by one old person: 'He was a man of the people; he was one of us'.

A community is more likely to cherish one of its own than to import with success the hero and heroine stories of other times and places. The collection of these stories about significant figures in the life of the congregation provides an insight into those images of faith which move the people to perseverance and hope. To honour them by reference on important occasions and in acts of acknowledgment is one way of binding a people closer to their shared confession.

What do the stories cherished by the people tell of the journey of faith? What hopes do they hold out? What ultimate concern do they reveal? These stories are not just stories. They designate those people with whom the congregation engages in an inner dialogue, a conversation which fashions its life. A running conversation with such people is what enlivens our spirits and gives us cause for rejoicing. It is also the way each of us learns to tell our own story.

'Who somebody is or was we can know only by knowing the story of which he is himself the hero – his biography, in other words everything else we know of him, including the work he may have left behind, tells us only what he is or was.'[7]

The stamp that leaves the mark 'Christian' is in the hero stories of the people. Interpreting what the hero stories tell and employing them creatively in the people's shared existence is a way of giving strength to the self-identity of the community.

ARTIFACTS OF SIGNIFICANCE

This particular focusing concept moves more in the category of space than the category of time. In the church in which I grew up there is a tablet which commemorates the ministry of a former minister who died after being speared by Aborigines. That slice of history is taken from the early days of white settlement in the local area, at a time when there was a throwing aside of the convict yoke. The land was being possessed for settlement, and territorial disputes with Aboriginal tribes inhabiting the area were inevitable. That testimony to the pioneer days of the congregation provided a frame of reference for its present responsibility toward Australian Aborigines.

Another such story comes from a congregation whose church was seriously damaged when a typhoon swept through the area. A decision was taken by the congregation to rebuild, a courageous decision in the light of the economic circumstances operating at the time. In the new building they incorporated timbers from the first building. Today when the story of the congregation is told, those timbers stand as a testimony of a generation of faithful people who trusted the future.

There are curious mementos in many congregations: the silver trowel that was used to lay the cornerstone of the building, a baptismal font sculptured out of a large boulder from the mines which once had given the town its livelihood; a framed charter from the Church of Scotland sanctioning the beginnings of a new congregation. To illustrate from the story of the Uniting Church in Australia, there are now in united congregations symbols and sacred objects that had their significance in former Methodist, Presbyterian or Congregational communities. A Catholic convent that undertook a ministry to homeless men, in its earliest days passed out food to the needy through a hole in the convent wall. Today the convent is still registered as the 'hole in the wall' charity. The hole remains in the wall even yet.

The historical phases of a congregation's life can be traced by identifying the times and events when various objects were located in the fabric of a building as an intention to affirm some significant event, person, or circumstance.

Each of these occasions made sense to the people because they were able to proclaim something fundamental about their faith. A local congregation, by learning to value its past and the struggles that the reading of the past discloses, can grow to an understanding of itself: a self grounded transparently in the power which constituted it, and which continues to feed and sustain its life.

The perspective that living history affords is one in which scepticism, despair and relativity are overcome. One student working in a congregation discovered in the story of the people fond recollection of two former members, sisters, who owned a bakery. It was their custom on occasions past to provide bread and cakes for gatherings of the congregation. On an appropriate occasion, the student baked a loaf of bread and, telling the story of the two sisters, distributed the bread to children and older members of the congregation. The people responded with joy and gratitude, some older members remembering and younger members learning of a period of recent history which, through the ministry of two of its members, had constituted the people as a community, sharers of the one bread together.

VALUING THE PAST: EDUCATIONAL POSSIBILITIES

There are times and occasions when the focusing concepts fulfil their task as described earlier. They can be used in a variety of settings 'to bring forth significance, convey meaning, restore symbols to life and call forth new symbols'.

Remembered history can be clothed in liturgical dress, and the story of the people enacted not only in the immediate past but back into the honoured traditions of the faith still yeasting in the people's lives. The link between past time and present time is forged effortlessly and with meaning.

Hero stories can be told to children, shared at retreats, celebrated on festival occasions. A former professor of mine would once a year interrupt his class and take them into the courtyard of the seminary where a bust of Horace Bushnell, the famed nineteenth-century Christian educator, stood. Many things were said, including the story of how Bushnell would read the morning newspaper to his children, interpreting it from a Christian perspective. It is in such ways that the stories of the faithful become our story. We are brought into contact with those influences which can direct our present course. For the story honours the flowing nature of historical experience and invites us to participate in the collective adventure of the life of faith.

No fund of stories remains intact forever in an original form. In retaining stories selections are made. In retelling them emphases and interpretation shift. They are reorganised to address the circumstances of the present. The biblical stories share this polishing, cutting and resetting as do all stories. But the valuing of the past through story, event and ritual puts the past into context with life. An organic sense is preserved, continuity ensured from a generation that went out into the night of God's calling and wrought a destiny by faith.

The artifacts of significance can be the means of leading people on pilgrimage around their own church buildings. Stations, not of the cross, but of the journey of a company of people can be identified. As the people pause at each point, memory is summoned and imagination employed to celebrate that vital sense of being caught up into events of significance.

It is in learning to value the history of a particular people and in owning or claiming that story that a community can be instructed and guided to an awareness of its identity in the present. Involving the people in the process of recovering their history and developing the forums through which it can be expressed is itself a significant educational enterprise. The meaning thus derived ensures that the people view their present circumstances not as fixed and given but as a drama which is still being played out to its end. That realisation itself leads to reflection and recommitment. It remains true that we shape ourselves by the story that our life tells.

NOTES TO CHAPTER 7

1. Panikkar, Raimundo. *Myth, Faith and Hermeneutics*, New York: Paulist Press, © 1979, p.8. Used by permission.

2. Seymour, Jack and Miller, Donald, *Contemporary Approaches to Christian Education*, Nashville: Abingdon, 1982, p.21. Used by permission.

3. ibid., p.22. The primary questions that this approach should address are: How is a prophetic word heard? How is the community itself transformed?

4. Niebuhr, *The Meaning of Revelation*, p.109.

5. Navone, John. *Towards a Theology of Story*, St. Paul Publications, 1977, p.13. Used by permission.

6. In *The Birth and Death of Meaning* Ernest Becker states the reason why he believes young people are no longer moved by the hero stories of their parents' generation. 'The crisis of middle and upper class youth in the social and economic structure of the western world is precisely a crisis of belief in the vitality of hero systems that are offered by contemporary materialistic society. The young no longer feel heroic in doing as their elders did and that's that.' Becker, Ernest. *The Birth and Death of Meaning*. Penguin Books, Second Edition 1971, p.130.

7. Quoted by John Navone, op.cit., p.71.

CHAPTER EIGHT

Claiming the Present

WHAT HAVE BEEN DESIGNATED AS *FOCUSING CONCEPTS* IN relation to the past can be employed with equal validity in the present. Focusing concepts are ways in which interpretation can be made of prevailing frames of reference. The force of the concepts, which function as a tool of education, is directed to bringing the people into intimate dialogue with the meanings existing in their shared story.

Three focusing concepts appropriate to the present are significant symbols, circumscribing imagery and rituals. In examining what these concepts offer in the task of interpretation, the present is always in dynamic interaction with the past and future. What exists, and in the form it exists, does so because it gives guidance and direction to people's lives. People create the reality they need in order to discover themselves. That statement needs to be corrected by a further observation. In the structure of experience which lies at the heart of a community self-conscious about its way, there are resources which are not generated out of any present moment but given to the people as gift, as generative possibility. That creative force, by means of the very historicity that holds it, is able to fashion genuinely new responses to contemporary events. The paradox cannot be avoided that we are made by and also make the symbolic systems that define us. The educational task requires of us that we take seriously the responsibility to create our own destiny, for faith and grace are most present at that point where we choose to 'sin boldly', in Luther's phrase.

SIGNIFICANT SYMBOL

There is a fertile and amusing passage in Donald Horne's book *The Education of Young Donald* which addresses the role of symbols.

'In the bottom right-hand drawer of his side of the dressing-table Dad kept the symbols of his most important beliefs. When there was no one in the house I sometimes took them out and wondered at them. There was his masonic apron, his Bible, his war medals, a bedouin's knife he had brought back from the Palestine campaign, an army revolver, his spurs. One day I put on the masonic apron and medals. Holding the revolver in my hand, with the bedouin's knife at my waist and the spurs on my feet, I looked at myself in the mirror and saw an Australian.'[1]

The symbols, as Horne observes, related directly to his father's most cherished beliefs, and integrated his personal story with the aspirations and hopes of wider communities, social and national. His son saw that constellation of symbols giving definition to his concept of 'Australian'. Such symbols conferred identity. It was identity cast in a particular heroic mould.

It can safely be said that few if any of those symbols today are normative for what passes as quintessentially 'Australian'. Symbols can live and die. They can also be reborn to serve a new age. Each generation calls forth its own, and claims some as fundamental to their self-understanding. The metaphor 'black is beautiful' was one such verbal symbol that integrated the collective consciousness of black Americans in the 1960s and 1970s in the United States. The root meaning of the word symbol is to unify and to focus. To understand the significant symbol or symbols of a people is to know much about them. For the meanings of a community are stored in the symbols they indwell. The symbols represent a level of reality that says, 'this is the way the world is'. It is the clusters of sacred symbols woven into some sort of ordered whole that is determinative for the view of the world held by those who participate believingly in that to which the total configuration points.

To refer again to the words of Mircea Eliade quoted in Chapter 5; 'The symbol reveals certain aspects of reality . . . which defy any other means of knowledge. Images, symbols and myths are not irresponsible creations of the psyche: they . . . fulfil a function, that of bringing to light the most hidden modalities of being'.[2]

It follows that symbols give rise to common experience and common action. They have the capacity to shape consciousness by relating present events and experiences to normative occasions and stories. The church of the present day shares, by and large, the same set of significant symbols with the earliest years of the Christian fellowship. The impact of such symbols is to confer meaning which becomes the basic character of shared consciousness.

The particular symbols of a community embody and express a more universal significance which, in its power to evoke response, engenders through the emotions it releases insight that can come to us in such fullness in no other way. Just as Adam can represent all humankind, so can Jesus be the embodiment of the New Creation.

It is the way of symbols that their special significance is interpreted by the context in which they are encountered, by the events that give them communicative space and by personal need. The existential and the normative become inter-related. That is why in searching out the significant symbols of the people a deliberate effort must be made to ensure that the symbols are closely tied to the social occasions and the common life of the people.

Conversation about symbols in congregations has revealed what is obvious enough, that although a church building may be filled with symbolic forms, not all of them are significant for the people. The full panoply of Christian symbolism might be to hand. Only those which strike a chord in the present experience of the community can truly be said to be significant at this point in their journey. What is meant by significant is the symbols' direct connection to present identity, its living influence on what is believed and done by the people. The eating of bread and wine may be constitutive of what being Christian means to one community. For another Christian fellowship it may have no essential relationship to being Christian at all.

One church building had over the doors as you entered the words 'Be you doers of the Word'. When conflict broke out in the church it was often negotiated by reference to these words. As a student working in the congregation noted, the people saw themselves essentially as a practical church which did practical acts of service. Their determining symbol was 'faithful action'. In another church building the words 'Worship the Lord in the beauty of Holiness' in large letters climbed up and down the arch spanning the sanctuary area. The minister of the church was confident that the congregation had internalised this understanding of themselves so thoroughly that the quality and tone of worship in the church was significantly more reverent than in the other congregations under his charge.

The meaning which is focused in symbols is released in the narrative discourse of the people's story and dramatised in their rituals which express what is commonly affirmed. The nature of the symbols vary. They can be territorial, generic, or organic symbols. Not all of them are explicitly Christian. Many are natural symbols, and there are others which are shared in common with a variety of faiths. A cross, swastika, interlocking circles, the star of David, banners and flags of saints such as St. Andrew are significant to people in a variety of ways. A burning bush is a warrant for the identity of one people, a ship at sea the warrant for another.

Similarly candles can be a symbol of devotion in one tradition and the sign of apostasy in another. At a church of my acquaintance the people identify themselves by the spire of their church. Along the street the Episcopalian congregation rejoices that their church is built to an English design and thus retains their link with Anglicanism. Saints who give their names to a congregation – St. Stephen's, St. Paul's, St. Peter's – also present the people with an archetypal pattern of faith and obedience. In one congregation the binding symbol of their identity was the parish fair which was held once a year. A working class congregation, they saw the fair as the expression of their most conscious gifts. The joint venture bound them together in a common allegiance. Rather than attacking the practice the student working with the congregation decided to link the parish fair to the liturgical life of the parish and reinterpret its symbolic meaning in the process of affirming its importance for the people. Anyone conversant with a Celtic cross will recognise in this decision an old strategy. The parish fair was viewed as an opening for ministry. To attack it as peripheral to true faith would have been to court disaster.

It is important to recognise that much of the formative educational activity in a congregation arises out of the careful nurturing of the people's significant symbols, and their employment in a wider context than their local habitat. This recognition is not just for the occasions of liturgical celebration. The folk festivals and occasions of common sharing which happen in any congregation are likely to be as significant in the formation of Christian self-identity as other more formal gatherings such as Sunday worship. An intelligent use of the people's own symbols is of primary importance in the task of educating them in the faith once delivered to the saints.

CIRCUMSCRIBING IMAGERY

In the previous discussion on the role of language it was suggested that the 'nature of the universe' is a function of the language in which it is stated. That implies that each community constructs a view of the world in the choice of words and seminal images the people use to describe reality. Language is both the source of freedom and insight and a limitation on freedom and insight. Each congregation treasures certain designations, certain phrases and sayings above others. The people are set within that perceptual, linguistic frame. Their imagery surrounds them. Gaston Bachelard says of the image: '[An image] takes root in us . . . It becomes a new being in our language, expressing us by making us what it expresses; in other words, it is at once a becoming of expression, and a becoming of our being. Here expression creates being'.[3]

The images of a faith community are directly but not exclusively connected to the Hebraic Christian story. Faith is a prime imaginer of our collective world and the Christian paradigm offers an horizon within which we imagine the world. The stories of faith excite imagination which creates those images which circumscribe reality. Within the associated images of a congregation many of its core meanings reside. The total configuration of images can embody a fundamental vision. That is why attention to the imagery living within the people's language is so critical.

The formative images of a people can be sought by attention to a number of linguistic forms. These include metaphors, proverbs, parables and paradoxes.

A metaphor usually exists as a command image. 'You are the body of Christ.' Each metaphor gives concrete expression of a complex of feelings and impressions that is difficult to express any other way. The metaphors of a community therefore select, emphasise, suppress, focus and organise features of the common life of the people. 'We are the soldiers of Christ.' 'The church is God's missionary arm.' 'You are a sacramental vessel of the love of God.' It is not difficult to identify such central metaphors. They make their appearance in pulpit and pew, in business sessions and study groups. A central metaphor is likely to be employed as the warrant for present commitments. 'You are called to be caretakers, stewards.' The first step therefore is a careful collection of the root metaphors that again and again are advanced as warrant for the congregation's life and work.

A second source of understanding is the conventional wisdom of the people which appears from time to time in proverbs and aphorisms. Proverbs generally do not provide a systematic general analysis but rather a cluster of insights into the people's stock of common sense. 'Look not upon the wine when it is red' may be heard in a Methodist congregation. An Anglican congregation may celebrate wine as 'the gift which gladdens the heart of man'. 'The family that prays together, stays together.' 'A giving church is a believing church.' One slogan in a congregation was 'the new morality sounds like the old immorality'. It could scarcely be said to be genuinely a saying of the people but it indicated the nature of the congregation's viewpoint. 'Christians are not perfect, only forgiven' has gained acceptance among some congregations. A systematic record of such proverbs and sayings helps to build up an understanding of the overarching image the people hold of themselves.

A third source of understanding is parables and stories and, in conjunction with them, paradoxes that the people acknowledge. It is not difficult to discover which of the parables of Jesus are living among a group of people. The full story may not be told but reference will be made to the lost sheep, casting your seed on stony ground, separating the sheep and the goats, and building on firm foundations. Apart from the biblical parables, however, there are stories told in the congregation that reflect a particular parochial point of view.

Conventional viewpoints are commonly represented in stories which have achieved the status of stating things the way they are. In one such congregation there was a story of a boy who was given the task of fitting a jigsaw of the world together. He did it promptly. When asked how he could do it so quickly he replied, 'there was a drawing of a man on the other side. When I got the man right, the world came right'. This story was used to reinforce a view of Christian mission as personal evangelism, and to support a rationale for disengagement from political involvement and the ambiguities associated with the economic-political axis of social experience.

In this connection the notion of paradox is revealing. It was observed in one congregation that much attention at parish meetings was given to scrutiny of personal behaviour by some congregational members. A decision to sell church land and invest the money at prime interest with a large firm known to be exploiting workers in the Third World was not seen as involving ethical considerations. A similar paradox was the designation a church gave itself as 'the friendly church'. Newcomers found the church congregation distant and cold.

A collection of these elements of language, metaphor, proverbs, aphorisms, parables and paradoxes, both verbal and actual, helped students to search out the circumscribing imagery of the people. The most useful result was to identify those things in the gospel and present experience that were left out, never addressed or forgotten. In one congregation it included the rejection of infant baptism although that was the accepted practice of the church denomination in question.

The unifying images of a congregation are always a little above the language of everyday conversation although intimated in it. The elements of comedy, tragedy and irony can often be detected and related to the presiding images which locate and nurture the congregation's present experience. It has already been claimed that to give a people a new language is to change their view of reality and themselves in relation to that reality. Perhaps the greatest gain of the focusing concept of 'circumscribing imagery' for educating purposes is that it helps identify where constructive intervention can be made. As has been said, 'if we cannot imagine we cannot foresee'. To work with the images of the people is to deal with those dimensions of the collective inner life which can be unified in the present in a most powerful way. The image, as Ezra Pound reminds us, is 'an emotional and intellectual complex in an instant of time'. It has the power to evoke commitment and free creative energies.

RITUAL AND GESTURE

There is no religious faith that exists without rituals of some kind, for the function of rituals is to give concrete expression to what is believed. As George Santanyana argued, there must be specific rites and specific myths that give meaning to the rites. No one can be religious in general.

Polanyi points out that what gives rituals their meaning is the myth they recreate. It follows that rite and myth exist together and each exists in the other as its only viable form. Myth has no form until embodied in a rite. A rite has no meaning without an informing myth.[4] The rituals of a people embody their stories, myths, tales, and explicit beliefs. The notion of gesture is introduced here also as a focusing concept because it can reveal something of the style of a people which speaks with equal power of their basic commitments. 'In the beginning was the Gesture' is one form of translation of the opening words of the prologue of the Gospel according to St. John.

In the rituals and symbolic gestures of a people, the world as lived and the world as believed and imagined are fused together. Word and act become one event. And at the heart of that coming together is the fundamental confession of the people. In a Christian community God, as known in Christ, is the content of the commitment which is embodied in our rites and myths, in our gestures and stories. Such rites and gestures accompany commonplace events as well as those events that occur in 'great time'. They can relate to changes in place, a state of being, to social position, and age.

It is common in many congregations to have rituals that send people from the community, say to serve overseas in a mission field, or because the income earner of a family is taking up a new job. There are also receiving rituals in which people are welcomed into a fellowship, their status clarified by a rite of inclusion, even if it is only the verbal answering of a question before the congregation.

Rituals (as distinguished from celebrative rites) are as necessary to our daily living as are ordering gestures which arrange and direct the relationships which we see as significant. The patterns of behaviour which we confirm corporately are shaped by those acts and gestures which tell us who we are and what we must do. Meetings are opened with prayer. A passage of scripture is read. Thanks are extended at appropriate times. Banners are unfurled. The colour of liturgical cloths and stoles changes. People are dedicated. Visits are made. Annual meetings take place. Seasons of fasting and prayer are honoured. Retirements are noted. Births are celebrated. Significant rites of passage such as graduation are enacted. Engagements are announced, weddings duly solemnised. Burials hold us still for a time.

In all of these common events a sense of right or proper distance from the commonplace is observed, which is the precondition of a sense of style and self-knowledge.

A newcomer to a parish can learn a great deal by noticing what the people take for granted, and how they go about ordering their corporate life. Sometimes the rituals are confused and to a degree self-contradictory. In one parish, harvest festival was honoured in the middle of the season of Lent. Most of the goods that made up the harvest display were purchased in local stores, and not a few of the items were already plastic wrapped and packaged. The essential idea of offering the first fruits of the harvest to God had been obscured by the progressive urbanisation of the congregation's life. But pointing out the absurdities only angered the congregation. However anachronistic it had become, the service was deeply rooted in their consciousness as a fundamental demonstration of their faith as a people dependent on God's benefits, and responsive to his grace. The season of Lent had no special significance for them.

One story related in class was that of a new congregation that had been started in a burgeoning housing development. The place of meeting was a utility hall that was used by a kindergarten during the day and various other groups at night. A study of the language employed in the congregation alerted a student to the fact that there was nothing in the environment of the hall to focus the congregation in its identity as Christian. The language he described as secular. No clear ritual patterns had been established, no formative gestures except a Sunday liturgy that 'lurched from hymn to prayer to hymn to sermon to hymn'.

The attempt to deepen the congregation's understanding of itself began with

112

a serious effort to identify what rites and symbolic occasions could break the culture of silence that had emerged. In this endeavour was the clear conviction that in ritual is to be found 'a greater meaning in ourselves, in our lives and in our grasp of the nature of things'. It involved an educational process of guiding the congregation to a public enactment of their story as a people of God, so that story and ritual celebration could bring them into conscious touch with that which, in their present circumstances, no tongue was able to tell.

The linking of faith with ritual occasions, and daily experience with liturgical enactment, ensures that a congregation grows more deeply aware of its own nature and tasks as a community. Where attention is paid to the rituals and gestures of a people much is uncovered that is otherwise hidden. Much that is of seminal importance can be identified and lifted up as a centring ministration to the whole congregation. In such ways can the present time be redeemed from staleness and lack of meaning. We are describing here a unifying process which integrates a multiplicity of elements into an organic whole infused with meaning. The unitive function of symbol, gesture and ritual in the process of acquiring a knowledge which is concrete and significant is of the most essential kind.

NOTES TO CHAPTER 8

1. Horne, Donald. *The Education of Young Donald*, Melbourne: Sun Books, 1967, p.57. Permission granted by Curtis Brown (Aust.) Pty. Ltd., Sydney.

2. Eliade, op. cit., p.59.

3. Bachelard, op. cit., p.xix.

4. Polanyi and Prosch, op. cit., p.154.

CHAPTER NINE

Seeking a Future

N
O COMMUNITY CAN EXIST WITH ITS MEANINGS INTACT THAT fails in some way to address the future, both in its particular and general aspects. The story of a people needs to be integrated with a wider cosmic frame so that past and present lead on to a purpose and destiny which overcomes and goes beyond the limits of time.

Three focusing concepts that have proved useful in searching out a sense of providential intent in a community are a myth of destiny held by the people, their images of hope, and the vision which impels their lives. Where no future is perceived a necrophilic mentality dominates. Without a perceived future, no community can continue for long to summon its energies to meet new tasks. It is in the way we address the future that we claim it, by the act of seeking a fulfilment of that which is promised.

MYTH OF DESTINY

In one class one of the students, a nun, decided to seek out the myth that had shaped her own religious community. When she had joined the Order it was a contemplative one, with members of the convent apportioned certain hours each day so that a perpetual cycle of prayer and adoration was maintained.

After Vatican II, radical changes occurred. The traditional habits were redesigned, a new name was chosen for the Order, the formerly closed community became open to contact with the wider community. A substantial alteration in lifestyle took place. The change from a contemplative to an open, serving style of life precipitated a crisis. Several members left the Order. Others stayed on but with much confusion and uncertainty. Reflecting on the history of the congregation the student realised that with the breaking of the old patterns had gone the sustaining myth which had given meaning to the life of the Order. No new myth had emerged that fused meaning and purpose with present events.

The community set about exploring its destiny as a eucharistic company whose life of brokenness and service existed as a living symbol of the sacrament of Christ. A new venture was begun among the poor. In the process the community began to tell a new story in which the commitment of the Order to justice and peace was to shape their future way.

'It is in story form that our feelings of the sacred are eventually symbolised. Our narrative consciousness compels us communally to experience events, places and persons in the context of some story or other.'[1] That is why the identification of the myth of a congregation, understood as its shaping story, is an important step in the process of interpretation. As Pannenberg claims, myth is the word that narrates, logos the word that orders.[2]

The language of a community, coupled with its symbols and rituals, spells out the essential understanding of their future. The myth tells of the inner meaning of things which cannot be conveyed in any other way. In Alan Watt's celebrated definition: 'Myth is to be defined as a complex of stories . . . which, for various reasons, human beings regard as demonstrations of the inner meaning of the universe and of human life'.[3] When a congregation says 'as in Adam all die so in Christ shall all be made alive' it is expressing mythopoeically a confession about the nature of the world. As Cassirer comments, 'the species is immediately present in the particular; in the particular it lives and works'. If Adam is the symbol of all people condemned, Christ is the symbol of all people redeemed. The words, 'Jesus lives', enshrine a mythology.

In one congregation studied by a class member the continuing refrain of darkness and light led him to an understanding of the people's story, a myth in which they lived in the light, while all around was darkness. The future was to be the arena for their justification when the present conflicts would be transmitted into joy, and victory achieved over evil. Another student detected in a congregation not a conflict-vindication scenario but rather an evolutionary consciousness in which the people along with all creation were growing to become that which would complete the purposes of God. Yet another story, binding on people's understanding, was a congregation's hope that their faithful witness would be the motivating force for a transformed human situation. In yet another the myth of the congregation was summed up in the phrase, 'to build the kingdom'.

It is not always the case that a myth is positively related to the essential meaning of the Christian gospel. I well remember a congregation where the absolute command was to pray. If no change occurred it was due to our lack of faith and hardness of heart. We were urged to pray harder still. The fault lay with the congregation's lack of faith. The relationship of the sustaining myth to the reality I experienced was totally false. It is an illustration of the fact that, like every other aspect of human life, myths can be corrupted and diseased. Equally negative and positive dimensions are part of the myth-making activities of a congregation.

The telling of a new story, the call to seek a new destiny, is as old as Abraham and as contemporary as any modern Exodus. So the opportunity for understanding the people's relationship to the future which is gathered into their myth of destiny is of crucial importance. What story commands the allegiance of the people? Where does it lead? In what way is the future dealt with in their corporate myth?

A myth is a way of apprehending the world. The vehicle of a myth is the story itself. The force of a myth, in Wheelwright's terms, is 'the vaguely looming significance'.[4] The significance mentioned here is not easily discerned for it is elusively present within the confines of the story itself. That is why the myth is most attainable in the gestures and ritual acts which bring the people into active communion with their story. The myth of destiny persuasive for a people can be explored most profitably in the context of rite and ceremony. The essential story of a community is discernible in its acts and achievements. These give direction to its odyssey and reveal the quality and temper of the spirit of the community in a particular and concrete manner.

Once identified it can be the source of much fruitful dialogue about the meaning of faith for their human journey. If it is true that we create the future to a significant degree by the way we conceive it, then the telling of a story riddled with overtones of destiny is a function of prophecy. Our faith struggles to make the future whole. The educative possibilities include a redefinition not only of personal identity but community direction. It is a way of helping a community sing a new song.

IMAGES OF HOPE

'If we cannot imagine we cannot foresee.'[5] Bachelard in one sentence gives powerful expression to the capacity of imagination to draw together in new projective formations the swirling impressions which are our daily experience. The imagery of hope in a congregation is a source of generative energy. It is more than 'a picture drawn by the fancy'; rather it is an expression of the faith held by a people in God's power to create a new thing. The Bible is full of such images of hope.

The promise is that the crooked way will be made straight, the lion and the lamb will lie down together, and people will turn their swords into ploughshares and war will be no more. There is hope that one will come to preach deliverance, set at liberty the captives, give sight to the blind, proclaim the acceptable year of the Lord's favour. The images are of the hungry fed, the naked clothed, the restoration of humanity, a new creation, a new Jerusalem. It is not possible to read the Scriptures without being confronted by the images of hope held out in the writings of communities centuries apart. The life of the church is a record of such expectation. God is creating a new earth and a new heaven. The power of such images is unmistakable. 'I have a dream' said Martin Luther King and mobilised his people behind multiple images of a new future.

As Chaucer wrote,
'Men may dye of imaginacioun
so depe may impression be take
. . . imagination bodies forth
the form of things unknown.'

Images can evoke a response that will issue forth 'in a single act compounded of spiritual insight and physical perception'.[6] Every local community has such images of hope which describe or portray in some form that which the people confess in hope. These images seek to represent what will be, and to tell the people what they will become.

A local community gains its strength from the pervasiveness of its shared images. An overarching idea can be sustained by such images and embody a fundamental vision of the people's shared existence.

Sometimes the force of a community's imagery is sustained by a fresh relationship between familiar images which creates a metaphor of extraordinary significance, or gives unexpected nuances to commonly held convictions.

At other times, the coalition of local circumstances and events with faithful reflection leads the people from the particular moment to a general consensus of their status as God's people.

During the period in which the Uniting Church in Australia was coming into being local congregations lived with the hope that unity would bring about a renewal of the church, for unity was expressive of God's will and purpose. The unity of the Uniting Church pointed beyond itself to a wider union.

In some congregations the strongest images of hope have related to a release from the oppressive circumstances of unemployment. An Egyptian Orthodox congregation lived with the hope that God would send them their own priest. Students found a variety of expectations in congregations. Some congregations put their trust in the present generation of their young people, who were a warrant of their parents' faithfulness. In other congregations, under the influence of the church growth movement, hope was centred in increased numbers. One congregation prayed earnestly for peace in the world and fashioned its life by the struggle to overcome the military consciousness of present governments.

It is possible to identify in some congregations a quiet desperation about their future. Ageing constituencies, falling income and declining attendance often eclipse all present hope so that meaning is confined to what has been done rather than to what will yet be. Dealing with this kind of situation represents a challenge to those who minister to dying or depressed communities.

In such cases it is possible to seek for current sources of hope, recreating for the people a sense of present significance. In prayerful reflection nostalgia can be hope. God who has blessed us in the past will not leave himself without witnesses in any generation. To serve our time is the demand of obedience. God will bring forth new shoots that will blossom from the stump of the old tree.

Part of the educational ministry to congregations in declining circumstances is the evocation of fresh images and new words to describe the present. In one exercise undertaken by students in a congregation self-addressed as a dying church, new possibilities were offered to a group of teachers in the church. One of the students recorded the following observation:

'Barbara said she was amazed at the sudden change in the meeting. It had started with their saying "it's no use" and had gone to sudden hope ... Altogether this was an exciting meeting and a whole new range of possibilities opened up for the church. In a sense it opened the parish up to opportunities of focusing on present needs in the district rather than past glories of the congregation. It will give scope for the development of a communal dimension to religion as adults will be talking through the meaning of common experience and sharing these with children rather than giving instructions. It will translate the meaning of giving service to others from stress on doing jobs to one of being with people.'

As students worked with the parish what was pictured as grey unchanging circumstances gave way to an unexpected ground of possibility. People in the congregation began to look for the occasions of new beginning.

Working with the images of hope resident in a community has the advantage of mobilising people behind projects they already see as important. Offering images of hope out of the resources of the Bible and the tradition is a way of calling forth a renewed commitment so that we accept responsibility for the futures we will live in, by responding faithfully to present need. Discovering images of hope in a congregation may well be one of the most creative steps a newcomer can take. The size and quality of our hope after all significantly determines what we can become.

VISION

'Vision permeates our thoughts, desires, interests, ideals, imagination, feelings and body language; it is our worldview, our sense of life, our basic orientation towards reality. Our vision gives rise to our character, to our style of life, to our tone of being in the world. Vision is the way we grasp the complexity of life; it involves the meaning and value that we attach to the complexity of life as a whole and to the things of life in particular.'[7] It is John Navone's contention that the experience of vision is fundamental to human life. Certainly no community exists without some foundational vision of its role and purpose.

In the nature of the case vision includes within its scope a projection which guides and directs the intentionality of a particular people. Vision, from this perspective, is a total configuration of meaning focused in expectation of what should be done, and anticipation of what can be achieved.

The foundational vision of the Christian community comes from its central confession about Jesus Christ. This foundational vision of the church, mediated through apostles, scripture and tradition, gives a structure to experience. The interpretation it contains about the created order affirms a total pattern by which each faith community seeks to live out its professed charter. This primal vision of God, and his action in the world, transparent in the life and death of Jesus Christ, is definitive and normative for Christian existence. It makes its appearance in each Christian community which both owns it and sends it forth. It is this foundational vision of Jesus Christ which gives specific form to our own vision of the world and our place in it.

Within a local community the particular expression of Christian vision includes possibilities and limitations. It can offer an openness to new and unexpected ways of being, or cramp creative expression by a dry and lifeless rigidity. One of the most disabling absences in the life of a community is a clearly articulated vision of its nature and mission. Where there is no vision, it remains true, the people perish.

'The New Testament presupposes an openness to the mystery of God and holds us responsible for the quality of our response to it in our personal vision of the world and of ourselves. We are judged by our vision. What we see, our sense of the world, discloses what we are. Similarly, what we fail to see discloses what we are not.'[8]

In employing the focusing concept of 'vision', an attempt is made to go beyond the myth of destiny, which often concerns only the pilgrimage of a particular community. It tries to coalesce images of hope into a picture which co-ordinates all dimensions of a community's expectations. A flawed and inadequate vision can be as damaging as no vision at all. To seek out the vestiges of a partial vision, or to baptise an incipient vision by naming it among the people, can have revolutionary results.

One of the students working with her religious order on the idea of vision found a common despair. Among many recorded comments were the following: 'I smell death in our future. I live in a present with the smell of death overriding'; 'I don't think there is a vision. It is blank'; 'I have no vision. I do not think there is a future'; 'I really don't have a vision for all of us, I'm just finding out who I am'; 'I would like to think our vision is serving the poor, but I don't see that happening'.

In reflecting upon the situation the student wrote: 'Circumstances and historical developments have brought our congregation to a sense of uncertainty regarding identity and direction. Our task I think is to rename the vision. The process I feel will involve sifting through the myth, the history, the heroines, the symbols and the rituals (of the community) because I think the material which will reshape our vision is potentially in those things.'

Her response was the development of an eighteen-week program which set out to focus the creative energies of the community by a process of re-telling their story in a way that addressed the future. The key to the mobilisation of the resources of the congregation was the organising concept of vision.

The problem of motivation commonly raised by religious professionals is partly due to the absence of possible futures which compel commitment and enlist loyalties. In seeking to define a vision which emerges out of a community's own history and story, there are energising forces which claim the effort and support of the people.

The central affirmations of a community's address to the future can be traditional: a suffering community, a serving community, a reconciling community, a community of the poor, a charismatic community, a teaching community, a missionary community. In the congregations studied over five years all of these determining metaphors were identified.

One congregation shaped its vision around caring for divorced, lonely, handicapped and isolated people. Its concern was to make space for one-parent families. The environment of more traditional congregations concerned for nuclear families, they believed, was not so congenial. The particular response arose out of a clearly defined need but was not contained by the need alone. The concepts of forgiveness and reconciliation so central to the Christian gospel were embodied in the community's struggle to be a welcoming and reconciling community, which celebrated the overcoming of darkness, pain and failure by the spontaneous accepting love of a redeemed people.

The force of the idea of vision as a focusing concept can be grasped by the simple process of answering one question. 'What does the community offer to its people as it addresses the future?' In the answer to that question may be found an opening for ministry of the most significant kind.

INTERPRETATION AS PROCESS

Not all of the focusing concepts employed have been useful for all congregations at all times. Congregations, like people, are at different stages of development and self-awareness. What is useful in one congregation may not prove useful in the next. What has been demonstrated, however, is the efficacious influence on a congregation of helping it seek to understand more completely the nature of its shared existence, and the struggle to deepen and enrich the essential elements of its life.

In all cases choices have to be made. Most of them involve conflict of some kind. But the very process of educating inevitably involves hard decisions. A choice for the new may mean a choice against the old. A choice for the new may only be possible because of a renewed choice for the old. There is no absolute rule that is universally valid.

It is important that the process of interpretation be undertaken in continual dialogue with the people, who are both the authors and the architects of what is conceived and acted upon. The role of the participant observer is not one of telling the people what they must do, but rather expresses itself in a dialogic encounter in which co-intentional learning enterprises are devised and carried out.

Just as naming is a necessary background to the process of interpretation, so interpretation leads to the phase of remaking guided by the identification of openings for ministry. The process of interpretation is carried forward into the active phase of remaking the culture out of its own generative sources. It is important therefore to underline again the ongoing nature of what is here described. The life of a congregation flows on, however it may be contained within the broad banks it has cut for itself. Whether it flows faster and cuts deeper, or redirects its resources over a broader area never before travelled, it must continue to move forward or decry its very being. At least as far as the life of the spirit is concerned, we are a travelling people.

NOTES TO CHAPTER 9

1. Crites, Stephen. 'The Narrative Quality of Experience'. *Journal of the American Academy of Religion*, xxxix, 1971.

2. Pannenberg, Wolfhart. *Basic Questions in Theology*, Vol. II, Philadelphia: Fortress Press, 1971.

3. Watts, Alan. *Myth and Ritual in Christianity*, 1954, p.7. This definition compares with another statement by Watts which is also instructive. 'Myth. A complex of images or a story, whether factual or fanciful, taken to represent the deepest truths of life, or simply regarded as specially significant for no clearly realised reason.' ibid., London, New York: Thames and Hudson, 1953 edition, p.63.

4. Wheelwright, op. cit. pp.148-149.

5. Bachelard, op. cit., p.xxx.

6. Tate, Allen quoted by Phillip Wheelwright in *Metaphor and Reality*, Bloomington and London: Indiana University Press, 1968, p.67.

7. Navone, John. *Theology and Revelation*, Cork: Mercier Press, 1968, p.116.

8. ibid., p.120.

PART FOUR
REMAKING

CHAPTER TEN

Remaking: the Reconstruction of Experience

THE THIRD MOVEMENT OF THE THREE-FOLD PROCESS WE ARE following, that of remaking, is a crucial one. What has been gained by analysis and unveiled by interpretation has now to be employed in an intentional way to reconstruct the experience of the community, beginning at those points where openings for ministry are perceived to exist.

One useful way of beginning that process is a projection of an overall image of the life of the community. In order to achieve this, within the confines of the course I have been teaching, students are asked to make a non-verbal presentation which brings together all of those nuances, hunches and conclusions that have begun to distil within them.

The results have been unexpected as well as instructive. One student, a Christian Brother, played the story of the Christian Brothers in Australia on his violin. Beginning with the founding hymn of the community the music recapitulated the history of the order to the present day when a reprise of the hymn was played, incorporating new elements. The last bar was slightly off key! Another student danced out the life of her community. Another represented his community through a juggling act. There have been clay models, dramatic mimes, string sculpture, and paintings. The range of media has been extensive.

But a common experience has been the gaining of an integrated perspective on the community they belong to and seek to remake. As these presentations are made to a group of their peers, the same group which has been sharing weekly reports through the second phase of interpretation, the attempt to verbalise what has occurred in the non-verbal exercise has been rich in meaning and productive in outcome.

A period of reflection follows each presentation in which conclusions are identified and a consensus sought about where the openings for ministry exist. The final phase is one in which action outcomes are planned that seem to fit the circumstances and need of the particular community under review.

THE PROCESS OF REMAKING – THE THREE-FOLD MOVEMENT

In the brief description above three phases have been identified which guide the remaking process. These are (1) imaging, (2) conceptualising, (3) re-imaging. A further explanation of each of these phases illustrates the logic that lies behind the choice of this pattern.

1. *Imaging*

Reference has already been made to Michael Polanyi's contention that we know more than we can tell. Much of our understanding of a congregation's life is not conscious. The meanings which guide and direct us operate at levels of our being which are not directly accessible to rational control. Concerning the most important things, we more often than not find our mouths filled with cotton wool when we seek to explain to others, or even to ourselves, why certain persons, concerns, values or beliefs mean so much to us.

From indwelling a congregation an intuitive sense of what is present within the community emerges which can make its appearance through forms which honour the affective dimension. The medium for expression, an image, is one appropriate to the way that intuitive knowledge is possessed. We are dealing here with a primary mode of knowing, an inscape of a particular, dependent perspective whose proper habitat is that of image.

There has been enough said already about the subtle shaping of our lives by the central images and root metaphors that indwell our social experience. It needs no repetition here. But some word of caution needs to be uttered.

Images can bring us to the threshold of new possibilities but they are constantly in danger of being destroyed before they can tell what they hold by an impatient desire to control their expression. As a deer can fill a forest with magic, and yet flee at the slightest sound, so the premature application of critical reason to a developing image can destroy what it has to offer before it has made its proper and unique contribution.

Many new paths have been lost because of an insensitive censoring of what has been offered because it seemed to lack common sense. But the very nature of imaging relates us often to meaning which only appears at the confluence of logical incompatibilities. Each opening for ministry is as much a child of intuition as the offspring of rational thought. We should not fear to go into the dark places for there we learn new things. Honouring the rhythm of the first phase, that of imaging, is an indispensable first step. Premature closure is to be avoided at all costs if the greatest gain is to be won.

2. *Conceptualising*

Charles Williams, the British author, was sharply aware of the ambiguity associated with images. Romanticism, he argued, was overly concerned with images in an uncritical way. Asceticism on the other hand rejected images as a source of knowing with a consequent loss of depth and vitality. Williams himself warned that in the affirmation of images a dialectical consciousness was necessary: on the one hand in the apprehension of the Holy in the manifold images of literature and life 'this is also Thou', and on the other hand, 'neither is this Thou'.[1] A critical distance is necessary to discern what is truly of importance in nascent imagery. We need both to reject and to affirm images.

Luther was equally blunt. 'Only a fool learns only from experience.' The exercise of 'graceful reason' is central to the process of harvesting what has been learned. The tension inherent in the second phase is more than the move from an affective to a cognitive style of processing the data. It is the infinitely complex task of bringing into conjunction the relative perspective of the present with the normative claims of the faith as responsive to scripture, creeds, tradition and formal dogmatics. The tension is the tension always present between the particular and the universal. The issue is a delicate matter of choice. 'Can we distinguish from among the profusion of ancient traditions the branches of the tree that should live and grow because they are the ones that bear the true Gospel fruit? Can we select judiciously what to transplant, what to prune and what to encourage in the new growth?'[2]

In the present discussion a deliberate decision was made to balance the triangle on its apex; that is, to begin from the concrete facticity of a particular community. That may be judged to be too precarious an enterprise to be maintained. However, it is from one fixed point that the lines of thought can travel to the basic universal propositions about faith. The danger of absolutising the relative is overcome by the exercise of critical reasoning that brings the particular experience of a congregation into dialogue with other voices and other times and thus saves the parochial spirit from isolation and distortion.

The correction of this second phase is necessary not only to ensure the presence of a critical principle that roots out distortions, obscurities, rationalisations and error, but also to ensure that the life of the local community remains open to new truth. A closed community squirrelling together its own truths and hoarding its life against the coming winter of the spirit is doomed to isolation and death. That is why the conceptualising phase is as critical a phase as any. The interpretation of what is gathered for consideration must test itself against a wider frame and in the light of what is normative and definitive for faith.

The period of conceptualising, however, is not without its own constraints. It must seek in its critical work to honour the experience of the people, respecting as far as possible the integrity of what is there. It must strive to be open to the multiple levels of meaning which are embedded in the story of the people. In its mediation between the present community and the fullness of the Christian heritage it must seek a creative balance. At the point of decision dialogue must occur that brings into sharp relief the tension between what is given and what is demanded, between what is and what is not yet, between what is struggling into expression slowly and painfully against what can be said with authority and precision. We should not fear to make mistakes since that is the only option we have.

3. Re-imaging

The third phase of re-imaging is guided by several concerns. The first is to seek to re-enter the culture, conscious of its claims upon those who serve it to recognise the fragility of its strength. The second is the guiding principle of openings for ministry. The third is the task of re-imaging, using the language, symbols, stories, hopes and fears of the people themselves.

On the first of these, the concern to set about intentionally to seek change, it has been found necessary to subject the suggested projects to the critical scrutiny of the people. Perhaps an image will serve to illustrate. In an art class when a student presents a drawing to the teacher, the teacher sees as the primary task the nurturing of the student's gift. He or she might well tear the drawing to shreds against accepted canons of style and excellence. But to do so is non-productive. Instead the student and the teacher sit down together, discuss, dissect, and then identify how the drawing may be carried on more creatively. Then the teacher moves back and gives the student room to act. In the local congregation the role of teacher and student interchange. Sometimes the newcomer is a student seeking help in developing a fuller picture. Other times, by helpful intervention, he or she offers creative suggestions, and then steps back as the community seeks to continue its work. The teacher-learner, learner-teacher interaction is guided by the recognition of mutual interdependence. Theologically it is an acknowledgment that gifts are given to the people of God which, called forth, can enable it to fulfil its responsibilities. Such gifts are not the possession of one person, lay or ordained. They are given to the community.

The second idea, that of openings for ministry, is fundamental to the thesis outlined in this book. The re-entry process, by which is meant an intentional decisive intervention into the flow of a congregation's life, is guided by the decision taken concerning openings for ministry. It is the intention to bring about change in a particular and defined way against a careful analysis of what is needed that justifies the claim that the processes of transformation are, in essence, educational. These openings can include opportunities for educational projects, liturgical celebration and reform, direct activities of mission and service. It is not possible to be precise about what will emerge from a process of analysis because it is a response to the particular dictates of local circumstance.

In one case, when the notion of openings for ministry was explored, it was decided that the first step was to do nothing. In the particular congregation a trade-off had been reached between the staff and the congregation. The staff were permitted to make all decisions. In return the congregation remained passive and was not expected to act on the decisions. The history of the congregation was one of continual frustration for ministers, who nonetheless still wanted control of the decision-making processes.

The judgment to do nothing was supported by a clear indication to the congregation that the body of Christ was not a ship run by a Captain Queeg seeking to control a mutinous crew, but rather a sharing community in which all made contribution. The decision to do nothing was an invitation to the community to seek new patterns of leadership, and to provide the space within which initiatives could find expression. In such a decision a re-imaging of styles of leadership was implied.

The third element, that of re-imaging as praxis, is related as much to style as to strategy. In the translation process we have described, from imaging to conceptualising to re-imaging, there has been an assumption that what communicates is what makes sense within the prevailing universe of discourse within a congregation. The language must relate to the present speech of the people. The symbols must be those that have currency within the congregation; the central metaphors, parables, and stories should engage the people not only in substance but in form. It remains a law of human relationship that people cannot move outside their own experience with any assurance. Where new words are used, liturgical reform undertaken, service ventures begun, they need first to be seen within the known in order to be given serious consideration. Where new symbols are confessed, or old symbols recovered, they should have a reference to those centres of meaning which define the identity of the people. This is not much more than common sense. As John Dewey argued, most innovative educative ventures fail because of a lack of continuity with past experience.

There is danger here that new ventures can be accommodated to the old environment and in that movement lose their direction and momentum. It is at this point that hard decisions have to be made. In one situation, after prolonged discussion and planning, several congregations of the Uniting Church agreed to unite in a new parish pattern. At the last moment when the crucial vote was held, the consensus fell apart and the motion was lost. The next Sunday the minister entered the pulpit in sackcloth and ashes as a sign of repentance. Here was a case where a normative judgment about the principle of unity was in direct confrontation with the expressed will of the people.

Circumstances arise in which prophetic gestures are necessary. In this case it was a protest within the present experience of the people and related directly to the situation of the communities concerned. It is more normal, however, for joint action projects to occur which have a claim for support because of their evident relationship to recognised need. Re-imaging is a transforming strategy relating the congregation to new areas of endeavour.

When English artists first came to Australia they painted gum trees like oaks and elms. For a community to recognise its own true environment it is necessary to offer new perspectives which acknowledge the difference between what is known and what is projected. Re-imaging is a delicate art of integrating old and new ways of viewing experience which permits its reconstruction in a comprehensive manner.

THE LOCAL CONGREGATION AS SUBJECT

The tension between what is normative for faith and the concrete reality of the daily routines of living in community can be recognised when attempts are made to give a precise definition of a local congregation. Take a definition of the Christian church, for example, like that of David Kelsey and make the subject of its reference a local congregation.

'A Christian community is a community of persons for whom the life, death and resurrection appearances of Jesus of Nazareth, taken as an interconnected whole, is at once: (a) the inauguration of God's promised kingly rule, (b) the promise of its full actualization eschatalogically, and (c) a call to live in the world with companions in forms of life (i) that are appropriate to the fact of the inauguration of the kingdom of God in precisely that peculiar way, (ii) that serve the community's mission.'[3]

It is apparent in this definition that a normative perspective has pre-eminence, so that the prescription of Christian community stands over all particular local gatherings as a school-master to a school assembly.

By way of contrast, when Nelson seeks to define the local congregation from the perspective of its communal reality he does so by beginning with the saying attributed to Jesus: 'Where two or three are gathered in my name, there am I in the midst of them'. His conclusion is:

'This communal reality is found in a self-conscious association of believers who are permanent enough in location to have face-to-face relationships with each other in a variety of situations and who are stable enough to function as a corporate group in carrying out their mutually developed plans and activities.'[4]

These shared activities, Nelson adds, involve worship, fellowship, education and social action.[5] It is apparent, however, by comparing the two definitions that for Nelson the existential reality of a congregation's life is of primary concern, a joining the class in the swimming pool so to speak, rather than standing on the edge watching for drownings.

Kelsey, writing as a theologian, rightly defines the task of theology as one of assessing the *fittingness* of the community's current action and speech to its defining mission, the *significance* of the current forms of speech and action, and the *truth* of the community's speech as judged by the canons of scripture and tradition.[6]

Nelson is concerned with the *bond* between people and the nature of the interaction, the *meaning* of the shared activities for those who belong, and the *quality* of the community's witness and life and its relationship to culture.

These definitions illustrate the tension which exists in seeking to reach an agreement between the perspective taken by theologians concerned for normative judgments and educators who struggle to give form to a congregation's life in temper with the realities of a particular, idiosyncratic community.

There is no way of escaping the difficulty of balancing the two perspectives, each of which, within its proper domain, has a indispensable task to perform. The church is a mixed body. There is no single way of looking at or understanding the culture of a congregation. Nor is there a single definition of what the church is which will command unswerving obedience at all times and all places. History can offer no absolute resolution of the paradox of the church, its greatness and its wretchedness. There is no frictionless docking here of a craft with a mother ship that is out of the influence of the earth's pull and free of its ever present ambiguities in some realm of outer space.

What is common, however, to both sides of the dilemma offers a possibility of an agreed area of negotiation. That commonality includes a recognition that the knowledge appropriate to faith is not a possession but an exercise of understanding in the actualising of obedient response. As Joseph Martos argues, the principle that should guide our intepretation is that '. . . ideas and experiences, thinking and doing, theory and practice mutually influence each other over the course of time'.[7] No final separation can be maintained, nor is such a separation desirable, because a community of faith knows itself not only in thought but also in action.

Further, as theology attests, God is both immanent and transcendent, involved intimately in creation as its ground and source, yet in no sense confined to it or defined by it in any absolute way. Therefore to take reality seriously and to struggle with the stuff of experience in order to encounter its 'inner infirmity' in Tillich's phrase is a task fundamental to the life of any congregation. In that process four facets of a congregation's life claim attention.

MARKS OF THE CHURCH

The four areas most addressed in the attempts undertaken to understand the culture of a congregation are worship, mission, education and authority. They are not only the source of existential questions, they relate to the 'esse' of the church. In some form or other they make their appearance in every congregation. They are the areas in which continuing questions can be pursued. Authority as a category, however, pervades all levels of the other three categories. While it is necessary to isolate it here for the purpose of discussion, its determining influence is to be traced in every facet of congregational life.

1. *Worship*

The central rituals of the local congregation are those associated with the public worship of God. Their importance cannot be over-emphasised for they offer an organising centre for the celebration of faith. It is generally agreed that rituals fulfil at least the following functions in the life of a community:

1) They establish the identity of the people and by their repetition create community;

2) They give an interpretation of daily life and help us move into it with meaning and purpose;

3) They give root and vision to the Christian journey because of their enactment of our fundamental meanings;

4) They sustain and transmit who we are to rising generations and provide the means by which we understand who we are;

5) They are useful in ordering the pattern of daily commerce through celebration, affirmation and rites of transition, providing an intensification of shared experience;

6) They address the holy and have their significance in response to that mystery which girds human existence.

In order to focus the search for openings for ministry in the remaking phase, course participants are given the following task: 'Prepare three liturgies developed for the congregation with an indication of how they address openings for ministry.'

Some illustrations will indicate how these liturgies are prepared.

'The liturgy of the church has both reflected and shaped the central myth. It seemed appropriate to use liturgy to address that central myth. The church's myth centres around comfort. At the end of my second term essay on the life of this church I commented: "The ritual fails to include the changing situations of the individual and the group – there is little mention of what God is involved in today ... in the church or its members."

"The (present) ritual expresses the idea that the Christian life is

133

individualistic, personal and static. It is comfortable rather than challenging. It is dull rather than vital. It is in danger of being set too far away from the real events of life. It is my understanding that such an 'institutional church' needs to be told again the story of faith and to redefine all that it is by that story." Thus I felt that the central myth of the church needed to be redefined and retold.'

A consensus identified by the student was that the congregation was largely without hope. The preparation of the three liturgies therefore attempted to address the situation of this congregation in the following ways:

'The first liturgy sought to replace the "dead church" image with the truth of the Easter message. The second liturgy was designed for the church anniversary and emphasised that God was involved in the total history of the church, past, present and into the future. The third liturgy sought to address the "comfort myth" surrounding the rituals of the church, by re-interpreting it into the means of developing a "living faith" – a faith which affects our ability to rise above circumstances, changing our way of life, our relationships . . . The third will be set in the context of the church's expectation of a new minister in January.'

Other liturgies prepared by students reflected the same correspondence between analysis, interpretation and the task of reconstruction. Not all liturgies related to public worship. The aim of a valedictory youth club service was stated by one student this way:

'To conduct a service of worship in the coffee lounge (where the original Methodist Church met from 1953) from which we farewell departing club members. To incorporate the predominant youth club symbol of the painted names on the rear wall and the recently completed front wall, names which represent present youth club membership. To affirm the relevance of the youth club ministry today.'

The liturgy developed was a sending ritual of considerable significance. The rationale for another liturgy was stated this way:

'This liturgy is designed to celebrate and affirm the past, in order to move with hope into the future. This need has presented itself to me primarily through the choir whose sameness in both membership and style of music symbolises stability and security. It provides escape from threatening or challenging forces. It symbolises who we have been in the past, what we are comfortable with. It therefore seems appropriate to help the people celebrate this past in order that they move more confidently into the future.

This liturgy would be celebrated on the occasion of the church's 80th anniversary, on a Saturday afternoon at a picnic ground. The whole community will be invited to participate. Preparation beforehand involves the encouraging of all participants to dress in period costume of the turn of century when the church was established. Musical instruments such as guitars, shakers, drums, etc. would also be brought along. Old photographs and relics from the congregation's past are also to be displayed. Some of the older members will share anecdotes from the church's life.'

The closing moment of the liturgy is instructive:

'A cake with eighty candles is solemnly lit, and from this a single candle in a holder is lit from the cake, representing the new year. The candles on the cake are blown out by an older member of the church and the single candle handed to a young person, who then leads a procession of the entire community singing Sydney Carter's hymn "One More Step" accompanied by musical instruments.'

These illustrations are taken from Free and Reformed Church traditions. However those within the Catholic stream of the church with strong liturgical practices have found that they have ready to hand resources which give new direction to worship even within firmly entrenched traditional liturgies.

Parish sensitivity to liturgical reform is well known to anyone who has served in a local congregation. Resistance to change, for change means a redefinition of deeply possessed convictions, can come as readily from pulpit as from pew. It is to be acknowledged that this strategy of remaking has revolutionary possibilities. Worship after all not only declares our understanding of God and our relationship to him, but determines the nature of our response to others. The risk, if risk it is, lies in moving too rapidly, before a new vision can be appropriated. Yet as Joseph Martos reminds us, speaking of the sacraments, rituals are human creations which function as doors to the sacred. 'For sacraments are not ends in themselves but means to an end. They are doors to the sacred, and so what really counts is not the doors themselves but what lies beyond them.'[8]

2. *Mission*

In turning to the issue of the mission of a local congregation the question raised by Thomas Groome concerning the innate conservatism of local cultures needs to be addressed.[9] It is Groome's concern that a commitment to a socialisation-enculturation model of education poses a massive danger that the church will remain locked within its own language systems, neither able nor wanting to address the issue of cultural transformation. The question he raises is 'what will save a congregation which is zealously engaged in a process of miseducation?'.

There are two kinds of questions here. The first, 'how can a congregation remain faithful?', 'What safeguards its life from distortion and apostasy?'. The second, 'how can conservative cultures address the surrounding environment in a responsible manner?'.

The first of these questions has had a response in what has already been said about the point of intersection between a particular social ethos and the normative judgments of the faith. Criteria that help in the negotiation of that tension include coherence, consistency, comprehensiveness and adequacy. The critical principle which shapes the catholic substance of the church is that which Tillich claims is the protestant principle, namely that nothing relative should be made absolute.

The correction therefore that is built into the present scheme relates to the movement within the phase of remaking. While affirming the general thrust of the socialisation explanation of the shaping and transmission of faith, the essential responsibility of interpreting the on-going life of a community by reference to orthodox descriptions of the nature of the church remains constant. To that degree it is more accurate to say that alongside the socialisation theory, that of education as interpretation carries equal weight in the processes offered here. The characteristics of the school of interpretation as outlined by Miller and Seymour are consistent with this claim.[10]

The second question is more difficult. A recurring theme from the work with local congregations is the attitude to forces outside its life, and how they are reflected in the story of the congregation. The typology world-denying or world-affirming has proved instructive as students have wrestled with the particular ways in which the mission of the local congregation is discussed. In many cases where the myth of a congregation is world-denying the culture remained closed and withdrawn from direct contact with social realities. Where the prevailing theological expression is world-affirming, then a more open stance towards culture in general can usually be detected.

The parochial spirit of local congregations needs to be informed by two perspectives on what being a Christian community requires. The first is that to be a genuinely Christian community a congregation must affirm that it is a community in which all are called to participate. That understanding of the church cuts across all distinctions of race, sex, age or economic circumstance. It transcends physical and mental disabilities, as well as social judgments.

To hold that understanding of the church before a congregation is not easy when a local culture gains its strength not only by the inclusion of some people but by the tacit, often unintentional, exclusion of other people.

A second major threat to congregational wholeness is the refusal of a local community to think and act ecumenically. The church confesses one Lord, one faith, one baptism. If a local congregation guides its life by an understanding of the oneness of the church, it is able to overcome many of its own parochial loyalties. It can be open, not only to the surrounding culture but also to other faith communities struggling to declare the Christian gospel within its own particular environment and circumstances. These two perspectives are of equal significance for the wholeness of a local faith community.

Congregations are almost universally located in the socio-religious axes of social experience. The political-economic axis is often proscribed because it involves political alliances and judgments and breeds dissension. If there is one single perplexing question confronting those working with local congregations it is how to effect a workable movement from the socio-religious to the political-economic axis of social and cultural reality. That issue is complicated by the circumstances operating in a congregation, referred to elsewhere as circumstances of deprivation, balanced uncertainty or affluence.

Two illustrations may serve to indicate how students have tackled this issue. One student decided that the most strategic way of addressing the issue of mission was through the liturgy, as a primary step for the development of projects related to the content of worship. The project was developed in the following way.

In conjunction with a national program in Australia called One World Week (similar to One Great Hour of Sharing), an action-oriented program for churches, a liturgy was developed under the title: *Discovering our Place in One World*. In conjunction with Ministry Sunday there was another liturgy: *Discovering Our Ministry in One World*, and in conjunction with Harvest Sunday: *Celebrating Our One World*.

The three liturgies were focused around the themes fellowship, mission and life.

In the first liturgy, by pre-arrangement, family groups rose and announced the origins of their family – Europe, Asia, Latin America, Great Britain. The ethnic composition of the congregation and society was thereby directly addressed. The focal point of the liturgy was the offering in which the common destiny of humankind was confessed. This service of worship was linked to a Friday evening educational activity. After exploring the One World concept in a variety of ways attention was directed to the question: 'Where are the nations of the world in *our* community; what is *our* response to them?'. Action programs were the intended outcome of the process described.

Pursuing the same theme of One World on Ministry Sunday, the worship of the congregation was linked to a Friday evening activity which preceded the Sunday service. The historical link of the church to St. Columba and his missionary work was investigated, with questions directed to its style and effectiveness. Children of the congregation were engaged in making a large replica of the Celtic Cross of St. Columba with arrows on each end to symbolise 'going out' into the world in the direction of the cross. The symbol was to be constructed of tactile material to add another dimension to its impact.

Symbols made on the Friday evening were carried into Sunday worship by the children, themselves a symbol of ministry in the context of the worship. The intention here was to introduce a common symbol (a variation of the St. Columba symbol positioned just over their heads in the sanctuary) incorporated into the Ministry Sunday symbol. The deliberate linking of the concept of missionary activity in the present with the central symbol of the congregation, a symbol that maintained continuity with the past activity of the church, illustrates the attempt to address the congregation at the centre of its sustaining myth.

In the case of the final liturgy the ideas of work, creation, the sharing of gifts and providence, gathered under the theme of life, was related to the celebration of God's providence and the confession that all should be fed.

While these liturgies may be criticised for their restrictions to the present environs of the congregations, their intent was to lay a foundation for directed activities that the congregation could pursue in fulfilling its sense of mission.

A second illustration is a parish educational program entitled 'The Lion has Roared' which was an attempt to test an hypothesis 'that biblically, justice is expressed in the language of the people and in a form that calls for and therefore enhances critical consciousness.' The program consisted of six sessions, commencing with an after-worship elective on Social Justice Sunday and continuing with four evening study sessions and one evening service.

The program had the stated aim: 'participants will be called upon to address their own social consciousness through the study of case studies from the contemporary social situation'. It was guided by the following conviction: 'It is vital that a feeling of mutual attention to the issues be engendered rather than an environment whereby some expert outsider could be seen to be berating the present commitment of the participants'. The program included Bible study as well as reflection upon contemporary social realities.

The final session considered action possibilities. As the student wrote: 'Changes in life-style, political action and commitments that have been made by others is always a source of interest and inspiration. To this end throughout the program suggestions for action will be made where relevant, e.g. employment offices, Ecumenical Unemployment Task Group. Part of the input for the final session will be a consideration of the Shakertown Pledge and the reasons for its formulation'. The stated intention was to develop a 'pedagogy of the non-poor', and the initiatives were the beginning of a process to widen the vision of the congregation to include biblical perspectives on justice. The location of the final session in a worship service was seen to be strategic.

These illustrations need to be understood as responses to the limits and possibilities of two particular middle-class congregations. They are indicative of the potential for change which flows from the application of the schema already outlined. The six categories outlined in the first phase – time, space, language, intimacy, consensus, circumstance – can exist as transformative categories. They can be employed in radical ways. The focusing concepts can lead to remaking ventures which significantly re-order the established patterns of the culture of the congregation. If the assumption is made that the congregation is a flowing, living, growing, expanding organism, then present limitations can be viewed as relative not absolute boundaries.

3. Education

It is to be underlined that in the assumptions held about educating a people of God the intentional process addresses both formal and informal modes of congregational activity. A concentration on formal curriculum, even to determined instruction of what the church believes, is not eliminated by what is suggested here. The difference is that formal educational ventures are decided on and prosecuted within the congregation in response to judgments related to the total system and the openings for ministry it provides.

That is to argue that educational programming that does not relate particular ventures of learning to the total configuration of congregation belonging will not significantly address the underlying patterns of value formation and images of faithful living that are impressing themselves on all who participate in the community. The subsidiary dimensions, the background patterns of structure and process, are to be the true guides to what is best undertaken in formal education projects. Ministry to children, youth, adults, intergenerational activity, can then feed back into what is largely invisible but ultimately determinative for the formation of faith. The focus on community as the enriching matrix for faith becomes of primary concern in the nurturing of faith.

Gestalt psychology offers a useful illustration of what is intended by this statement. Our experience of the world according to this school of thought is developed into a picture in which there exist foreground and background elements. The prominence and location of foreground is dependent upon the influence and location of background. What holds meaning for us is the relationship, the configuration between these two dimensions. Significant learning is associated with bringing much that is background into foreground, and moving attention from foreground elements which then merge into background.

This interplay between foreground and background is instructive in considering the formal educational activities of the local church which occupy our focal attention. If they are related congruently to the total matrix of a congregation's life, and can merge into the patterning of the community's life, their force and relevance is considerably enhanced. A connectedness between intentional, systematic educational programs and the total worshipping, witnessing life of the community ensures that the inner and outer aspects of the life of the congregation are congruent and unified.

It is not difficult to discover in many local congregations a separation between Sunday school, youth clubs or sporting groups which largely constitute formal activities with the youth of the church, and the central liturgical acts of the community. Often there is a tenuous link between these organised programs and the centres of meaning which distinguish these pursuits as related in a direct way to a Christian confession.

Because of the dialogic nature of the process in seeking to educate a people of God, it becomes a matter of necessity that those who undertake teaching responsibilities within the congregation be involved in the conversations concerning the life of the congregation, and the task of renaming.

Not all traditions lend themselves to this focus on teaching as a community responsibility as readily as those churches in the Reformed tradition where the concept of 'teaching elders' is still maintained. A group – here termed elders – within the congregation accepts the responsibility to ensure that the whole congregation remains in conversation with the essential formative sources of faith. This responsibility is undertaken in relation to pastoral and administrative concerns as well as those strictly defined as educational.

If the circle of elders in a congregation becomes the reflecting guiding centre of the task of renaming, there is every chance that projects proposed will be intimately related to the life of the people, and undertaken with responsibility by those who have already committed themselves to be caretakers of the health of the community. The model of teaching elders has its analogues in other traditions. But whether within the formal structures of congregational life, or with informal groups, a continuing dialogue is necessary as the reconstruction of congregational experience takes place. It needs only to be added that to continue to preach, teach, and serve a faith community without paying attention to the relationship of those essential tasks of ministry to the substantive elements of meaning present in the life of the people is like sailing a yacht without reference to the conditions of wind or water. More often than not the result is a people becalmed or in danger of going under, bewildered as to why nothing that is done seems to make any difference.

4. *Authority*

The reference to teaching elders and to the need for dialogue between clergy and lay people raises a difficulty about authority within a congregation. Patterns of authority in any congregation can be determined by a number of factors. These include the sacramental tradition of the people, the view of priesthood, local autonomy in tension with centralised decision-making, quality of leadership, patterns of governance.

There are limits and possibilities in each tradition whether broadly conceived as Catholic, Reformed, Orthodox or Free Church. It is common in some traditions for the authority of the priest or minister to be coterminous with ordination. The ordained leader speaks ex-cathedra on matters of faith, and has exclusive control over all matters of liturgical practice. In such cases the people's freedom to respond and assume responsibility is limited to specific areas of church life.

These are traditions within the Christian family where authority is not invested in the office of priest but shared collectively by the people. In cases of this kind the freedom of the clergy is correspondingly restricted. There is no one pattern of authority that can be established as sacrosanct for the Christian church. Branches of the church have variously answered the question about authority whether Catholic, Orthodox, Anglican, Reformed or Free Church.

The essential question that can be raised over all traditions is whether the principle of dialogue is accepted or rejected in leadership patterns. Where no commitment to dialogue with the people exists then the suggestions offered here are likely to be of limited value. Unless those who have responsibility within a congregation listen to the people, in order to serve them more adequately, then the structure of experience within a congregation, which is the believing environment of the people, may well remain unknown. The very mystery buried at the heart of a faith community may not be visible, the centres of meaning eternally elusive to those who seek to minister to and with a particular, unique, and complex people of God.

The sharpness of the question about authority is not only a question about the exercise of power, the need for control, or judgments about right order. It has to do with issues related to style of ministry, internalised images of 'priest, pastor or prophet', openness to new possibilities within the minister-educator and the congregation as well. It is to be regretted that much of the church's work in theological education implicitly assumes an isolated and singular role function for ordained Christians which reinforces a strong independent or loner psychology in theological students. Part of the pain associated with the transition crisis from seminary to parish is the reluctance to share authority and the fear of giving up power. The need for control often becomes a deeply entrenched imperative. For many, self-actualisation and role performance are so intimately related that a question about the function of ministry is received as a personal assault. There is little freedom possible in role performance because the present established pattern is the warrant of personal identity. Where that complicity is cemented by the authority of respected theological traditions, it can be the most tragic of marriages for priest and people. Only genuine communication is adequate to produce a community of hope and purpose.

THE ROLE OF RESIDENT THEOLOGIAN-EDUCATOR

One consequence, and at first both an unexpected and an unwelcomed consequence, of struggling to engage a congregation in the manner described, is the crisis of identity it precipitates in many students. The nature of the threat is often traced to a rigid understanding of the role of minister or priest. It seems necessary therefore to enlarge the understanding of the role of minister, priest or pastor to include within it a definition of role which includes a designation such as theologian-educator. To keep these two aspects of ministry separated is not in the best interests of pulpit or pew. The plea inherent in this claim is more than a pious hope. Jesus himself was an educator of an extraordinary kind. He commanded his disciples, among other things, to teach. Therefore some of the requirements of that command need to be constantly addressed.

In the process of educating a people of God there are a number of ways of defining the educating task. The root of the word education is 'e-ducere', literally to lead forth or to bring out something which is potentially present, although not yet visible. Within this general rubric the educative task as offered here is precisely this loving struggle to call into full expression the communal life of a particular people.

In that task the minister, teaching elders and other members of the congregation may fulfil a number of quite specific roles. These include resident guide, instructor, facilitator, architect, planner, interpreter, resource person, analyst, counsellor, even in the modelling of new directions, the initiator of new trends. These particular designations are facets of the overall task of calling forth the people into a deeper expression of their shared existence. In one phrase, which has both theological as well as educational lineage, the call to be a teacher is the call to be a shepherd of being.

The Reformed tradition has cherished the work of Christ in the three-fold designation, prophet, priest and king, the latter being interpreted as meaning suffering servant, and thus to the serving role of pastor, which contemporary church practice reads as exercising pastoral care. The designation of teacher (rabbi), which is the predominant mode of address to Jesus by his contemporaries, is missing as a continuing thread in the fabric of the ministry of the ordained. Yet the dimension of education is present in all facets of ministry whether addressed directly or not. A considerable advantage in recovering this obscured dimension is that the theological reflection of the church will be related directly to the existential realities of the life of faith as it attempts to act out what prayerful reflection has understood and integrative thought articulated.

BY WAY OF CONCLUSION

The attempt to develop a master key to the local congregation, which has been a subject of concern for some six years of my teaching life, has been an attempt to seek a renewal of the local congregation by taking seriously what is both present and absent in a particular faith community. It has assumed that any system or method of control must of necessity omit certain factors which can be sources of vitality within congregational life. It has been an attempt to escape the trap of a limited focus on foreground matters and, to employ an illustration from photography, to move from a narrow focus to address background reality which encompasses infinity. It has meant placing a high premium on the unknown, and being open to surprise. It has followed a connection about the mystery of God's action and its effects which are wonder and awe. And it has cherished the insight that a process cannot be understood by stopping it but only by stepping into its current. Understanding must move with the flow of the life of a congregation, must join it and grow with it. It is an affirmation that God moves within the life of people struggling to be obedient to their calling. It affirms that revelation is the coincidence of event and meaning which proclaims the presence of God's redeeming activity in the midst of human ambiguity and struggle.

That it has consequences for individuals and for congregations can be summed up by a passage from a letter a student wrote with her final paper.

'In being a participant-observer of my community, using the six categories as a basis for analysis, I began to understand my people. In learning to understand them, to accept them and in accepting them, to love them. This has been accompanied by the desire to share more intimately in their lives and to contribute to the life of the community in a more significant way. This yearning has come at a time when my formal theological education is almost completed and the question of vocation one of immediacy. The need to discover my gifts and abilities, my niche in the church community, and an authentic style of ministry has become suddenly more pressing. Until this year I had not recognised just how important Christian community was to me.'

There has been considerable evidence to suggest that the schema outlined here has been and can be useful. That judgment can only be sustained however where an attempt has been made to use it to unlock the hidden doors of a community's life. That is a process of seeking to uncover God's gracious presence, a process which, properly understood, is none other than an active meditation upon Paul's own generative image, 'You are the body of Christ, and severally members of it'. To know that we are part of Christ's body in word and deed and life is the goal of the enterprise. It is a way of seeing and living by faith. For if a congregation is alive it will share the characteristics of all living things and bring forth new possibilities. These in their turn recreate us again, and call us to go on with both meaning and purpose. In such a fashion does God make available those resources that shape, form and sustain a community of faith.

NOTES TO CHAPTER 10

1. Williams, Charles. *War in Heaven*, Victor Gollanz, 1930.

2. Gelineau, Joseph. *The Liturgy Today and Tomorrow*, New York, N.Y./Paramus, N.J.: Paulist Press, 1978, p.9. Published and copyright 1978 by Darton, Longman and Todd Limited, London. Used by permission of the publishers.

3. Kelsey, op. cit. p.386.

4. Nelson, Ellis. op. cit. p.98. See also 'Why this insistence on the communal nature of the Church? Because it is by this process that faith can be incubated and nurtured. Faith is a concomitant of human association. That is why the Church must be a gathering of Christians which is permanent enough to allow individuals to know each other in various facets of their life and regular enough in its meetings to be able to develop a sense of solidarity in Christ and their mission to the world. The human interaction is the most powerful process we know for creating and sustaining values, affections, commitments; for shaping a distinctive style of life; and for commanding loyalty greater than life itself.' (p. 101)

5. ibid, pp.102-20.

6. Kesley, op. cit., p.392.

7. Martos, Joseph. *Doors to the Sacred*, New York: Doubleday and Company Inc., 1981, p.7. Copyright SCM Press, London. Used by permission.

8. ibid. p.531.

9. Groome, Thomas. op. cit. p.126. Some of the difficulty Groome identifies is present in his own formulation of praxis. In accepting Hegel as a surer guide than Marx, his use of the idea of the kingdom of God is constantly in danger of being separated from the reality of experience. Groome is well aware of this, but in employing his method of praxis within a school environment the notion of praxis becomes domesticated to that environment and, as a consequence, loses much of its radical designation as employed by Freire. The rationale for this restriction is the nature of middle class society in America, a far different social and political environment to the situation Freire is addressing in Latin America or Africa. But the danger is apparent. The kingdom of God becomes a pious ideal. Christian religious education remains confined within the environment of conservative structures which eschew the political, economic issues. This dilemma in Groome's impressive struggle is one which continues to bedevil most present attempts to take the local church seriously and work within the limitations of its present social and policital loyalties. Of course this generalisation has particular exceptions.

10. Seymour, and Miller, op. cit. See Chapter 6: 'Faith, Seeking Understanding Interpretation as a Task of Christian Education', p.123.

APPENDIX I

Work Sheets for the Task of Naming

*T*HE FOLLOWING WORKSHEETS ARE INTENDED TO BE USED AS A guide to personal reflection as well as for group discussion. It has been found useful to keep a journal during the period of investigation. The intention of the journal, much like that of a writer's notebook, is to record impressions, anecdotes, phrases or events that seem significant, even if the reason for that significance is not immediately clear. The following schema can help organise scattered bits and pieces of knowledge and integrate them into a holistic image of the life of the people. Much of the usefulness of the sheets rests on the intuitive reflection and lateral thinking of the participant-observer as he or she seeks to fit together a picture from many suggestions, hints, and subtle clues.

TIME:
* What is the predominant sense of time in the congregation?
* To what events and rituals is it most immediately linked?

above time

behind time————— NOW ————ahead of time
TIME

below time.

* List in each quadrant those words, events or acts that seem to you to locate the congregation in that area.

* Do these references relate to a particular theme (e.g. age, circumstance)?

* What does the clustering of references suggest to you?

SPACE: * What are the sacred locations in the congregation's life?

* On what particularly significant occasions do they relate to that space? Where are the thresholds of
  – auditory space (note the points of significant change)
  – visual space
  – tactile space?

* Take a plan of the church grounds. Colour code it in relation to the category of space, using your own code and criteria. What does it tell you about (a) centres of meaning, (b) communication patterns?

LANGUAGE: * What are the key words and phrases used by the people to describe their life together?

* What are some key biblical words and concepts that are absent?

	Biblical	Non-Biblical
Verbal Symbolic		
Non-Verbal Symbolic (list this in a phrase or denoting symbol)		

What language would you regard as super-imposed language?

From the above listing what conclusions can be drawn about the language of the congregation and its present function?

INTIMACY: * Intimacy as closeness: How is this expressed?

     * Intimacy as depth: What is essential to the people as ultimate claim?

     * Intimacy as commitment: To what causes, projects, visions are the people committed?

Draw a circle with the centre symbolising the most intimate, the periphery the least intimate. Link inner and outer points with three lines. At points along the lines register what you believe is the case for the congregation, using the three dimensions of intimacy: closeness, commitment and depth.

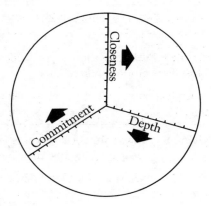

CONSENSUS:

      as **Nurture:**   What is cherished? What neglected?
                            What is affirmed? What rejected?
                            What is included? What excluded?

      as **Mission:**   Who is addressed? Who is ignored?
                            Is focus local, national, international?
                            Whose interests are most served?

as **Authority:**   Who has control? Who has little say?

Who exercises power? Who are power-less?

Who makes decisions? Who has no participation in decision-making?

List the most deeply held norms of the congregation along a spectrum.

|_____._____._____Worship_____._____._____|

|_____._____.____Education___._____._____|

most firmly |_____._____.___Mission___._____._____| least held
held norms   or of no

|_____._____.___Authority___._____.____| interest

If norm stated positively – restate it negatively

If norm stated negatively – restate it positively

Which norms in your judgment are a less than adequate statement of a Christian perspective?

CIRCUMSTANCE: List those factors which collectively describe the circumstances of the congregation.

* Deprivation:

* Balanced uncertainty:

* Abundance:

How are the prevailing circumstances negotiated by the people? Which of these elements are judged:
(a) immutable,
(b) beyond present power to change,
(c) can be changed,
(d) are under threat,
(e) need to be defended,
(f) are inevitable?

What can be done in your judgment to address the circumstances of the congregation (a) from the biblical tradition/Scriptures, (b) by way of education, (c) by concerted action?

APPENDIX II

Work Sheets
for the
Task of Interpreting

VALUING THE PAST

A. *Remembered history/actual history*

What makes what is remembered history meaningful to the people?

B. *Hero stories*

Who are the heroes/heroines? What paradigm of faith do they offer? How would you describe what they represent to the people?

C. *Artifacts of significance*

What are they? What significance is attached to them by the people?

CLAIMING THE PRESENT

D. *Symbol/s*

What is the central symbol in the people's identity as a people? What symbols are important in their life? Which carry most weight?

E. *Circumscribing imagery*

What are the central images, metaphors, parables of the people? What is their claim on the people's allegiance?

F. *Rituals and gestures*

What are the central rituals and gestures? What do they tell of the people's shared life and confession? What do they offer as source and ground of faith?

SEEKING A FUTURE

G. *Myth of destiny*

What is their myth of destiny? What does it offer? What does it neglect?

H. *Images of hope*

To what do they relate? Are they realistic or impossible hopes? Does the distinction matter?

I. *Vision*

What is the vision that guides the people? Is it a biblical vision? What are the sources of the vision?

What does a reflection on the above tell you about the centres of meaning which create the people as a community?

APPENDIX III

Work Sheets for the Task of Remaking

*I*N THE PROCESS OF REFLECTION ON THE COMMUNITY YOU ARE involved with, it is helpful to identify openings for ministry against a grid which draws attention to necessary elements in the life of faith. One such is offered here as a provisional guide.

OPENINGS FOR MINISTRY

1. *Worship*
   - shape of liturgy
   - Christian festivals
   - rituals of inclusion, sending
   - patterns of participation

2. *Mission*
   - action projects related to:
     local community
     national interests, concerns
     international awareness and action projects

3. *Education*
   - nurture
   - instruction
   - action-reflection
   - spiritual formation

4. *Authority*
   - nature of authority
   - style of authority
   - patterns of decision-making
   - mechanisms of control
   - flexibility and capacity to respond to change

The *Openings for ministry* as conceived need to be directed to the outer surface of congregational life but shaped by and responsive to the centres of meaning that are the sources of faith. In the formation stages it is useful to ask:

(a) Who can most creatively respond to my interpretation?

(b) Who will most be affected by change? How can they be invited to participate in the process of change?

BIBLIOGRAPHY

Alderfer, C.P. and Brown, L.D. *Learning From Changing: Organizational Diagnosis and Development*, Beverly Hills, California: Sage Productions, 1975.

Bachelard, Gaston. *The Poetics of Space*, translated by Maria Jolas, New York: Orion Press, 1964.

Becker, Ernest. *The Birth and Death of Meaning*, New York: Penguin Books, Second Edition, 1971.

Escape from Evil, New York: Free Press, 1975.

Bentzen, M.M., et al. *Changing Schools: The Magic Feather Principle*, New York: McGraw Hill, 1974.

Berger, Peter L. *The Heretical Imperative*, New York: Anchor Press/Doubleday, 1979.

Black, Max. *Models and Metaphors*, New York: Cornell Uni. Press, 1962.

Borhek, James T., and Curtis, Richard F. *A Sociology of Belief*, New York: John Wiley and Sons, 1975.

Brueggemann, Walter. *Living Toward a Vision*, Philadelphia: United Church Press, 1976.

Bruhn, Severyn. *The Human Perspective in Sociology*, Englewood Cliffs, N.J.: Prentice Hall, 1966.

Buber, Martin, *Between Man and Man*, translated by Ronald Gregor Smith, London: Kegan Paul, 1947.

Burgess, Harold William. *An Invitation to Religious Education*, Mishawaka, Indiana: Religious Education Press Inc., 1975.

Cameron, W.G. *Toward Dynamic Equilibrium: An Inservice Approach to Organisation Development*, Sydney: Division of Services, Inservice Education, N.S.W. Dept. of Education, 1978.

Carnell, Corbin. *Bright Shadow of Reality: C.S. Lewis and the Feeling Intellect*, Grand Rapids, Michigan: William B. Eerdmans, 1974.

Cassirer, Ernst. The Philosophy of Symbolic Forms, Vol 3: *The Phenomenology of Knowledge*, translated by Ralph Manheim, New Haven: Yale Uni. Press, 1957.

Cox, Harvey. *The Seduction of the Spirit*, New York: Simon and Schuster, 1973.

Dunne C.S.C., John S. *A Search for God in Time and Memory*, Notre Dame, Indiana: University of Notre Dame Press, 1977.

The Way of All the Earth, New York: The Macmillan Company, 1972.

Eliade, Mircea. *Images and Symbols*, translated by Philip Mairet, London: Harvill Press, 1961.

Freire, Paulo. *Pedagogy of the Oppressed*, translated by Myra Bergman Ramos, New York: Herder and Herder, 1971.

Geertz, Clifford. *The Interpretation of Cultures*, New York: Basic Books, 1973.

Gelineau,, Jospeh. *The Liturgy Today and Tomorrow*, New York: Paulist Press, 1978.

Groome, Thomas H. *Christian Religious Education*, San Francisco: Harper and Row, 1980.

Gustafson, James M. *Treasure in Earthen Vessels*, New York: Harper and Row, 1961.

Heidegger, Martin, *Discourse on Thinking*, translated by John M. Anderson and E. Hans Freund, New York: Harper and Row, 1959.

Horne, Donald. *The Education of Young Donald*, Melbourne: Sun Books, 1967.

Kierkegaard, Søren. *Philosophical Fragments or A Fragment of Philosophy*, Princeton, New Jersey: Princeton Uni. Press, 1962.

Knox, John. *The Church and the Reality of Christ*, New York: Harper and Row, 1962.

Lewis, C.S. 'Bluspels and Flalansferes', *Rehabilitations*, London: Oxford Press, 1939.

   God in the Dock, essays on theology and ethics, edited by Walter Hooper, Grand Rapids: Eerdmans, 1970.

Martin, David. *The Breaking of the Image*, New York: St. Martin's Press, 1979.

Martos, Joseph. *Doors to the Sacred*, New York: Doubleday and Company Inc., 1981.

Meland, Bernard E. *Faith and Culture*, London: Allen and Unwin, 1955.

   Fallible Forms and Symbols, Philadelphia: Fortress Press, 1976.

Moran, Gabriel. *The Present Revelation*, New York: Herder and Herder, 1972.

Navone, John. *Towards a Theology of Story*, Slough: St. Paul Publications, 1977.

   Theology and Revelation, Cork: Mercier Press, 1968.

Nelson, C. Ellis. *Where Faith Begins*, Richmond, Virginia: John Knox Press, 1967.

Neville, Gwen Kennedy, and Westerhoff III, John H. *Learning Through Liturgy*, New York: The Seabury Press, 1978.

Niebuhr, H. Richard. *Christ and Culture*, New York: Harper, 1951.

   The Meaning of Revelation, New York: The Macmillan Company, 1941.

Ornstein, Robert E. (ed.) *The Nature of Human Consciousness*, New York: The Viking Press Inc., 1974.

Pannenberg, Wolfhart. *Basic Questions in Theology*, Collected Essays, Vol. II, translated by George H. Kehm, Philadelphia: Fortress Press, 1971.

Polanyi, Michael. *Personal Knowledge*, Chicago: The Uni. of Chicago Press, 1958.

   The Tacit Dimenson, New York: Anchor Books, Doubleday and Company Inc., 1967.

Polanyi, Michael, and Prosch, Harry. *Meaning*, Chicago: The Uni. of Chicago Press, 1975.

Potok, Chaim. *The Chosen*, New York: Simon and Schuster, 1967.

Ricoeur, Paul. *The Symbolism of Evil*, translated by Emerson Buchanan, New York: Harper and Row, 1967.

Rudge, Peter F. *Ministry and Management*, London: Tavistock, 1968.

Schleiermacher, Friedrich. *The Christian Faith*, ed. H.R. Mackintosh and J.S. Stewart, 'The translation has been executed by various hands', Philadelphia: Fortress Press, 1976.

Schutz, A. 'The Stranger', *Studies in Social Theory*, ed. A Brodersen, The Hague: Martinus Nijhoff, 1964.

Seymour, Jack and Miller, Donald. *Contemporary Approaches to Christian Education*, Nashville: Abingdon, 1982.

Tillich, Paul. *The Dynamics of Faith*, London: George Allen & Unwin Ltd., 1957.

Troeltsch, Ernst. *The Social Teaching of the Christian Churches*, Vol. I, II, London: George Allen and Unwin, Ltd., New York: The Macmillan Company, 1931.

Turner, Victor Witter. *Dramas, Fields, and Metaphors*, Ithaca: Cornell Uni. Press, 1974.

   The Ritual Process, New York: Cornell Uni. Press, 1969.

Watts, Alan. *Myth and Ritual in Christianity*, London: Thames and Hudson, 1953.

Westerhoff III, John H. *Will Our Children Have Faith?*, New York: The Seabury Press, 1976.

Wheelwright, Phillip, *The Burning Fountain*, Bloomington: Indiana Uni. Press, 1968.

Metaphor and Reality, Bloomington, Indiana Uni. Press, 1968.

Wilson, Monica. *Rituals of Kinship Among the Nyakyusa*, London: Oxford Uni. Press, 1957.

Yaker, Osmond, Cheek. *The Future of Time*, Hogarth Press.

Basic Issues In Theological Education, Theological Education, Vol. XVII, No. 2, Spring, 1981.

Blumer, Herbert. 'What is Wrong With Social Theory', *American Sociological Review*, Vol. 19, February 1954.

Crites, Stephen. 'The Narrative Quality of Experience', *Journal of the American Academy of Religion*, XXXIX, 1971.

Kelsey, David H. 'The Bible and Christian Theology', *Journal of the American Academy of Religion*, Volume XLVIII, Number 3, September 1980.

Mbiti, John S. 'Theological Impotence and the Universality of the Church', *Third World Theologies*, Mission Trends, No. 3, ed. Gerald H. Anderson and Thomas F. Stransky, C.S.P., New York: Paulist Press, Grand Rapids: William B. Eerdmans Publishing Company, 1976.

Meland, Bernard E. 'Faith and the Formative Imagery of Our Time', *Process Theology:* Basic Writings, ed. Ewart H. Cousins, New York: Newman Press, 1971.

O'Collins S.J., Gerald. *Theology and Revelation*, No. 2, *Theology Today*, General Editor: Edward Yarnold S.J., Hales Corner, Wisconsin: Clergy Book Service, 1968.

Tillich, Paul. World Perspectives, No. 9, *Dynamics of Faith*, London: George Allen and Unwin Ltd., 1957.